ANTI-CAPITALISM
The new generation of emancipatory movements

Ezequiel Adamovsky
Illustrated by Ilustradores Unidos
Translated by Marie Trigona

Seven Stories Press
New York

A Seven Stories Press First Edition
First English-language edition, May 2011
First published in 2008 by Era Naciente SRL in Buenos Aires, Argentina

Seven Stories Press
140 Watts Street
New York, NY 10013
www.sevenstories.com

College professors may order examination copies of Seven Stories Press
titles for a free six-month trial period. To order, visit
http://www.sevenstories.com/textbook or send a fax on
school letterhead to (212) 226-1411.

Book design by Carolina Katz and Jeremiah Boncha

Library of Congress Cataloging-in-Publication Data

CIP Data on file.

Printed in the USA

9 8 7 6 5 4 3 2 1

The anti-capitalists

Anti-capitalists are those of us who feel that much of the suffering in the world is the result of an unjust *social system*: *capitalism*. Even though many men and women have resisted this system since its formation, many centuries ago, only in the past 200 years has this resistance become *conscious*. Since then, in many places, in many ways, anti-capitalists have struggled for a different kind of society.

SOCIALISM

REVOLUTIONARY SYNDICALISM

ANARCHISM

MARXISM-LENINISM-TROTSKYISM-MAOISM

SOCIALIST FEMINISM

PEASANT MOVEMENTS

NATIONAL LIBERATION MOVEMENTS

GUEVARISM

AUTONOMISM

GLOBAL RESISTANCE MOVEMENT

ZAPATISTAS

RADICAL ECOLOGY

In order to understand anti-capitalism, first we need to understand capitalism.

What is capitalism?

More than anything, capitalism is a *social system*. That is to say a *way* of organizing social life. For people to be able to live together, society must accept the same "answers" to a series of "questions."

These "questions" can be answered in many ways. A *social system* is the set of "answers" that organizes a society. Throughout history, human beings have organized social life in many ways. Capitalism is just one of these *historic systems*, and it is fairly recent: it began to develop some 500 years ago.

An oppressive society

Throughout history there have existed many societies with different degrees of *equality*. However, capitalism is an *oppressive social system*. A system is oppressive when there is a group of people that has power over the rest, and they permanently retain that power. Power means having the capacity to persuade other people to obey and to do certain things, even things that cause them suffering. The "oppressed" may obey the "powerful" *because they are forced to*, although generally they obey because the *culture* in which they were educated taught them they should obey because it is the correct thing to do, or that it is the only way they can survive. There are different kinds of oppression, according to how power is distributed among people.

There is gender oppression, for example, when males exert power over women, making women work for them, when women receive unequal pay and benefits for their work, or when women are coerced to behave in ways that please men. This form of oppression, called patriarchy, has existed in almost all of the past social systems, and it is still predominant today.

Other forms of oppression can be established between ethnic groups, for example, when whites dominate blacks, Christians dominate Muslims, or one nation dominates another, just by the fact that they are considered *superior*.

A classist society

Capitalism is an oppressive *class* system. This means that there is a class of people—the *dominant class*. Because of the dominant class's position and attributes (or those they are said to have), they have the power to *dominate* everyone else. This is not to say that under capitalism the other forms of oppression have disappeared: class oppression can be combined with *racial* or *gender* oppression, to reinforce oppression.

Class power can be *instituted* in many ways; furthermore, it can be justified and organized through a series of institutions, norms, habits and ideas. In the Middle Ages, for example, feudal lords were considered *noble* due to their birth line and were given the duty of protecting the population from wars; this is why peasants had to pay taxes or work for them for free.

In India, it was believed that certain people who were considered descendents of gods had more importance than others, which is why they formed part of a superior caste. The inferior castes had to serve their superiors.

In the Soviet Union, officials and political leaders affirmed that they had the *knowledge* and *authority* to run society, and which is why they should occupy a privileged rank.

In all cases, society had developed a system of institutions, norms and beliefs to organize, legitimate and protect the *dominant class's* power. However, the *capitalist* class's power is *instituted* in a new way. Capitalist society is the first in which dominant class's power is not defined by birth right or by being a member of a closed group, but is fundamentally (although not exclusively) defined by the *economic* differences between people.

Social classes under capitalism: the bourgeoisie

The *dominant class* under capitalism—called the *bourgeoisie*—is defined by the amount and type of *economic resources* that they control.

The bourgeoisie gain *ownership* of the means of production through the *possession* of *property* such as land, companies, machines, money, banks, etc. However, often the bourgeoisie can control economic resources without necessarily being *owners*—for example, when corporate stocks are sold to thousands of small shareholders and only a group of big businessmen *control* the company.

To secure control over economic resources, the bourgeoisie need to control other areas: certain political offices, academic posts, the court system, and mass media, among others.

The dominant class is then defined as a group that directly or indirectly controls society's fundamental economic and noneconomic resources. Through this control they gain power over everyone else.

Another distinguishing characteristic of capitalism is that classes are not separated in only one instance and permanently; class lines are *fluid* and the separations between them *do not appear to be sharply defined*. Even though there is an undeniable division between people who control fundamental resources and those who do not, classes seem to be divided into a blurred *continuum* of degrees of wealth that range from the wealthiest to the poorest without clear "steps." Even though only a small number can occupy the position of the dominant class, each individual is led to believe that it is always possible to rise *up the ladder*.

9

The lower classes

Often, anti-capitalists debate these questions fervently, because they suppose that each individual acts according to the class that he or she belongs to. Were this true, identifying one's class and one's class allies would be crucial in developing political actions. To a certain degree this is true. But at the same time there are examples of people who have made political decisions that don't correspond to their supposed class position: professionals and shopkeepers have become revolutionaries, and workers have been conservatives.

In fact, aside from the *dominant class,* distinguishing other social classes can be tricky, if one thinks of class divides as fixed *categories.* Capitalism *is not a static system* characterized by class division. On the contrary, it is a *constant and everyday process* of separating people into different classes.

Separating people into classes is a mainstay of capitalism: it is a machine that divides people and prevents them from acting together. Other than the *minority* of the population that *directly* benefits from oppressing others, it doesn't make sense for people to outline class differences as if we actually *were* compartmentalized into set categories or separate entities.

Of course, workers, peasants, students, self-employed people, etc. exist, and each group has undeniably unique characteristics that affect the ways in which they perceive the world and relate to politics. However, it is important to focus on what they have in common and what can unify them, rather than identifying the differences that separate people into *warring classes*. Without a doubt, there are social groups that are more "comfortable" than others and can escape some of the suffering that the system causes; and maybe that's what causes them to have less radical opinions.

CAPITALISM AFFECTS ALMOST EVERYONE, IN VERY DIFFERENT WAYS. IF WE USE THE DEFINITION OF CAPITALISM THAT ACCEPTS A "CLASSIST" DIVISION OF PEOPLE, THEN WE'D BE DOING A FAVOR TO THE SYSTEM!

IN FACT, PEOPLE DO NOT HAVE TO BE DIVIDED INTO CLASSES: THAT IS ONE EFFECT OF THE SYSTEM. UNDER THE POWER OF THE DOMINANT CLASS, THERE ARE NOT ONE, TWO, OR THREE CLASSES TO DIVIDE PEOPLE INTO. THERE IS A MULTIPLICITY OF HUMAN LIFE.

Class struggle: capitalism's inherent crisis

As a *class society*, capitalism carries the burden of a permanent tension: *class struggle*. Just as oppression and exploitation are present in every corner of society, *resistance* is also present. Capitalism implies not only economic exploitation, but also stripping people of their ability *to act*, of their freedom of movement, the possibility of making autonomous *decisions* about how they want to live their lives. But at the same time, capitalism faces a constant resistance, a struggle to escape exploitation and oppression, and to recover the ability to act and decide freely. *Class struggle* is a constant battle between oppression and the urge to free oneself from it. Struggle may be present in varying degrees of consciousness, visibility or "volume", but it is always there.

Class struggle is when a worker goes on strike, but can also include when a worker quits a job to find a less exploitive workplace. Class struggle can manifest in a great rebellion, but can also be a slow and wary effort. Collective and conscious actions also make up struggle—for example, an ecological campaign against a company polluting the environment—but can also include individual and unconscious actions, like a young person seeking out a career that allows him or her to be independent (or rather, not to become a salaried employee).

Class struggle *requires* capitalism perpetually to develop new methods to oppress, exploit and divide, because the oppressed are constantly discovering new ways to organize, escape oppression and gain spaces of freedom.

CLASS STRUGGLE IS THE MOTOR OF HISTORY.

Karl Marx
(1818-1883)

This is why the dominant class's power tends to be unstable and fragile, making it necessary to *reinstate* itself every day. Capitalism is a system that exists in *permanent crisis*. Although there are specific technical explanations, *we* are the cause of the periodic economic crisis that the system suffers, through our efforts to escape, resist and rebel against capitalist power.

Private property

Under capitalism, the dominant class *institutes* power through a series of belief systems and institutions that permanently change, adapt or collapse due to class struggle. However, some institutions remain relatively stable. One of the most important is the idea that some global resources can be *private property*.

Property is private when someone has deprived or prevented others from using a specific resource.

Private property isn't a new concept; since the beginning of time people have retained the *exclusive* rights to certain assets: pieces of land, work tools, etc. However, under capitalism this right has extended to include almost everything. Thousands of acres and even lakes can be *private property*, along with ports, businesses, songs, ideas, genes or millions of dollars in a bank. Some people can *acquire* for free the few things that are still not privatized. For example, a company can pollute the air that belongs to *everyone* and occupy our visual space with advertisements. Capitalism is a privatizing machine.

Commodities, salary and market

Another fundamental institution of capitalism is commodities. Commodities are everything that is produced to sell to make profits. The purchase and sale of goods in a space called a *market* existed long before capitalism. However, capitalism has expanded the reach of the market enormously, and now almost anything can be bought and sold. A fish or a pot can be bought and sold, but so can health, education, information and safety. In order to access anything that has been *privatized*, one must *purchase* it. Even people's *time* has been transformed into a *commodity*.

An employer can purchase a worker's *time*, to employ for his or her own benefit, in exchange for a worker's *salary*. The difference in the *value* of what the worker produces with his labor and what the worker receives as a *salary* is what is called *surplus value*. Under capitalism, the *dominant class* appropriates the surplus value produced by workers and society. .

In precapitalist societies, the dominant class was happy with taxing or demanding a payment from the rest of the population, without trying to control their *time* as well. Under capitalism, the dominant class doesn't "make" anyone pay taxes, or work for a salary.

THE "OBLIGATION" IS INDIRECT: PEOPLE WHO HAVE BEEN DENIED RESOURCES HAVE NO OTHER CHOICE THAN TO HAND OVER THEIR TIME LABORING "VOLUNTARILY" FOR THE DOMINANT CLASS SO THEY WILL RECEIVE ENOUGH PAY TO PREVENT THEM FROM STARVING TO DEATH.

THIS OBLIGATION, WHICH APPEARS VOLUNTARY, IS WHAT IS CALLED ECONOMIC COERCION.

Karl Marx

Capitalism can be defined as a series of customs, laws, political and economic institutions and an entire *culture* that guarantees and legitimizes the fact that some people can *prevent* other people from accessing most resources, then *use* those other people to accumulate wealth for themselves. By controlling the *labor* of others, the dominant class produces *goods* to sell afterward in the market. This is how capitalists make profits that allow them to *accumulate* more wealth to maintain and amplify their *power*.

The "original accumulation"

Before capitalism, most men and women controlled their own *means of production*—land, animals and work tools—or they collectively shared them with neighbors. During this time, no one would have accepted selling their *time* to another person in order to survive: there was no *need*.

In this age, time and labor were not considered *goods*. This is why in order for capitalism to be established, an extensive process had to be carried out: the expropriation of the means of production, the wealth of entire nations, and the people's ability to live according to their own decisions and customs.

This process of expropriation is called *original accumulation*. In historic terms, it meant, among other things, the expulsion of thousands of peasants from their land in Europe and other places, which forced them to become salaried workers.

During the following centuries, *original accumulation* also took the form of colonialism, which implied the looting of world resources, the imposition of bloody colonial governments, and the annihilation of entire ethnic groups which resisted enslavement, etc.

Some believe that *original accumulation* was an inaugural stage to capitalism, a sort of stepping stone. Others view capitalism as a long and constant process of *original accumulation* that will end only with the demise of the capitalist system. In either case, it remains clear that capitalism is a social system that is *founded* on violence.

A global and expansive system

Even though capitalism arose in Europe only five centuries ago, it quickly spread throughout the entire globe; its *expansive logic* seems to have no limits.

The possibility of expansion is crucial for capitalism: it's the system's way of resolving its *inherent crisis*. Without expansion, it would simply collapse.

Nation-states

Throughout history, capitalism has expanded, creating institutions and social customs that previously did not exist. Some of capitalism's first creations were borders and *Nation-States*.

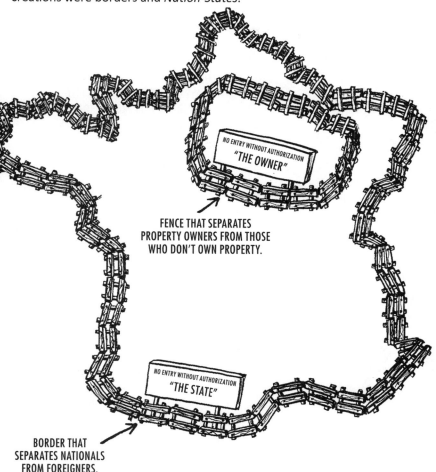

NO ENTRY WITHOUT AUTHORIZATION
"THE OWNER"

FENCE THAT SEPARATES
PROPERTY OWNERS FROM THOSE
WHO DON'T OWN PROPERTY.

NO ENTRY WITHOUT AUTHORIZATION
"THE STATE"

BORDER THAT
SEPARATES NATIONALS
FROM FOREIGNERS.

Capitalism invented the notion that a single political authority should *perfectly coincide* with a clearly defined geographic space outlined by *borders*; before, such a notion did not exist.

Capitalism also introduced the new idea that spaces *occupied* by a State must coincide with a *Nation,* or a group of inhabitants with a homogenous culture and identity.

> IN THIS WAY, CAPITALISM IMPOSED HOMOGENOUS LANGUAGES, COMMON LAWS AND CUSTOMS FOR POPULATIONS OF THE WORLD THAT PREVIOUSLY LIVED IN ASSORTED CULTURES AND HAD DIVERSE CULTURES AND WAYS OF LIFE. NATIONALIST IDEOLOGY IS A PART OF THIS PROCESS. ONLY A FEW CENTURIES AGO, NATIONAL IDENTITY DIDN'T EXIST.

Eric Hobsbawm (1917-)

The nation also implied that inhabitants would be divided into *separate* "national" territories. When a person crosses a border, they become foreigners and lose many of their rights. The labor of *standardization* and the simultaneous *division* of people brought centuries of war and *State violence*.

> I'M FRENCH AND I WILL DEFEND MY FATHERLAND UNTIL DEATH.

> I'M A LANDOWNER AND I WILL DEFEND MY LAND WITH MY LIFE.

Capitalism invented nation-states to establish a *unified internal market* that businessmen could exploit without restrictions. Nation-states were also useful in keeping the *population under better control* and to make the most of opportunities for colonial *expansion*.

Imperialism

A second course of expansion crept toward the "undiscovered" world during the 15th century. Through *imperialism* and *colonialism*, the new capitalist nations seized huge territories and forced inhabitants to act at their service.

Motivated by the promise of newfound riches, capitalist authorities and businessmen looted gold and silver from the Americas, enslaved millions of Africans, exploited Chinese workers, expropriated land from peasants in India and committed many other injustices for more than 500 years. The trade companies along with the dominant nation-states were the main institutions that led this expansion.

Imperialism also produced worldwide *uniformity*. For example, colonial powers tried to *assimilate* natives, forcing upon them European culture and languages. In addition, people were *divided* according to their nationality, religion or skin color. All nonwhites were now considered "inferior", and apt to be exploited and enslaved. The age of *imperialism* was also marked by wars, state violence and enormous suffering for most of humanity.

Globalization

The third stage of capitalist expansion is the current phase, which some call *globalization*. Economic globalization means a higher degree in the integration of production on a global scale; each part of a product is manufactured on different sides of the globe and the companies are organized *transnationally*.

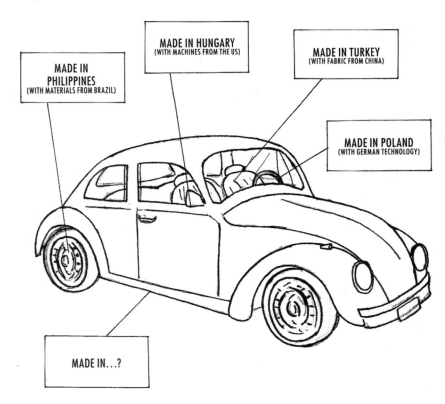

MADE IN HUNGARY
(WITH MACHINES FROM THE US)

MADE IN TURKEY
(WITH FABRIC FROM CHINA)

MADE IN PHILIPPINES
(WITH MATERIALS FROM BRAZIL)

MADE IN POLAND
(WITH GERMAN TECHNOLOGY)

MADE IN...?

By this time, *imperialism* and nations have already fulfilled a large part of their objective, and new institutions have been developed to intensify capitalist expansion. *Investors* and *transnational companies* need to move freely without being affected by *national borders*, which is why it is necessary to *standardize* certain rules for economic operations throughout the world, and to implement *cultural standards* for all nations.

Nation states no longer have enough power to carry out this task, and have, therefore, begun to lose power. To complement nations, private and (supposedly) public transnational institutions have been created to regulate and organize life on a global scale.

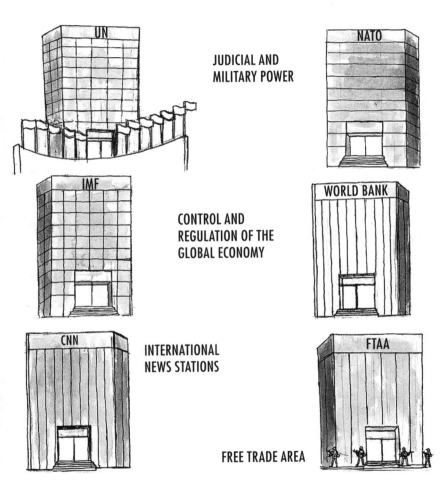

JUDICIAL AND
MILITARY POWER

CONTROL AND
REGULATION OF THE
GLOBAL ECONOMY

INTERNATIONAL
NEWS STATIONS

FREE TRADE AREA

Some authors, like Michael Hardt and Antonio Negri, maintain that capitalism is being "de-territorialized" and turning into a global *Empire*, where distinctions between the *center* of power and the periphery are increasingly blurred.

Internal Expansion

Capitalism has not only expanded towards the *exterior*—it has also expanded deeper into the *interior* of regions that are already capitalist, intensifying its presence even more. Rivers and seas, plazas and parks, schools and universities, theaters and entertainment, all are becoming increasingly *commodified, privatized*, and invaded with *advertising* in every corner, all dependent on sponsors.

Increasingly, there are fewer attractive and safe *public* spaces, which is why people are being forced to opt for *private* and *commercial* spaces. Something as simple as a walk in the park or down Main Street is being replaced by a trip to the *shopping mall*.

Capitalism has also *invaded natural spaces* and *products,* which are now being replaced by private and "artificial" ones. Natural seeds that anyone could plant are now being replaced by transgenic seeds that must be purchased from a laboratory. Farms have become "egg factories" or "vegetable factories." Capitalism has also increasingly penetrated *our minds* and *private lives.* We must work *harder* and for *less pay,* and even use our free time to produce *profits.*

I'M SUCCESSFUL, I'M SUCCESSFUL, I'M SUCCESSFUL...

Heavy workloads and hectic professional lives leave us with fewer opportunities to develop our personal lives. The dictatorship of consumption, fashion and status obliges us to consume in a specific way and leads us to make certain lifestyle choices (for example, what career to pursue) and conditions children from infancy.

Expansion—external and internal—is fundamental so that capitalism can survive its *permanent internal crisis.*

The State?

One of the most difficult aspects of capitalism to understand is the State and how it works. Anti-capitalists have never seen the state as "neutral," but rather as invariably taking the side of the dominant class.

THE STATE IS THE BUSINESS COMMITTEE OF THE DOMINANT CLASS.

Karl Marx

WE AGREE ON THAT, KARL. THE STATE IS A FUNDAMENTAL INSTRUMENT OF OPPRESSION.

Mikhail Bakunin (1814-1876)

Doubts over the role of the State began to surface in the 20th century when governments implemented "welfare" policies. Workers began to view the State as an institution that could introduce important laws for their benefit, including laws that went against the interests of the dominant class. The debate over the role of the State began to intensify, and it continues today: to what extent does the State *depend* on the dominant class? Does the State have some degree of autonomy?

Confusion in this debate comes largely from accepting the liberal distinction between State and society, as if they were two separate things. It is good to distinguish the two and their effects to gain a better understanding; but we must not forget that the State is an integral part of a capitalist society.

Guaranteeing accumulation

The *function of the State* has at least two aspects: guaranteeing long-term economic *accumulation* and assuring the system's *legitimacy*. Without the State, individual capitalists couldn't ensure the continuous *accumulation* of profits. For example, operating on their own, without State *regulation*, fishing companies would overfish until all the fish disappeared from the ocean.

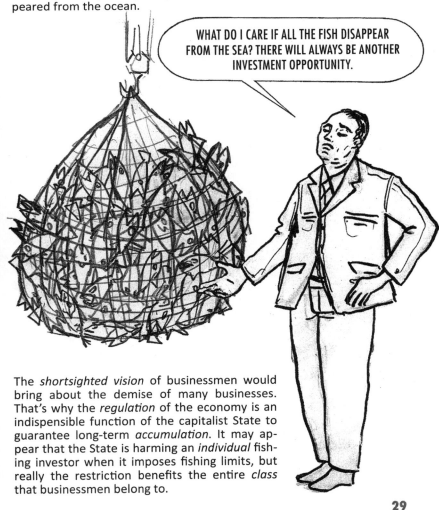

WHAT DO I CARE IF ALL THE FISH DISAPPEAR FROM THE SEA? THERE WILL ALWAYS BE ANOTHER INVESTMENT OPPORTUNITY.

The *shortsighted vision* of businessmen would bring about the demise of many businesses. That's why the *regulation* of the economy is an indispensible function of the capitalist State to guarantee long-term *accumulation*. It may appear that the State is harming an *individual* fishing investor when it imposes fishing limits, but really the restriction benefits the entire *class* that businessmen belong to.

Ensuring legitimacy

Because capitalism is permanently threatened by class struggle, the State is also in *charge* of ensuring that capitalist society is perceived as *legitimate*. If the majority of people consider the *system as illegitimate*, capitalism would easily collapse. When *legitimization* fails, the State is also in charge of *repression*. However, no system can survive long if it is based *only* on repression: the State always needs to ensure *legitimacy* for the capitalist society.

THE TWO FACES OF THE STATE...

This is why the State needs to maintain at all costs the *appearance of neutrality*. Even though the State is capitalist through and through, it needs to appear *independent* and *autonomous* from pressures of the powerful elite. As a consequence, the State on many occasions dictates laws that put its own interests at risk in the short term. This *appearance* of neutrality sometimes confuses people who try to understand how the State operates.

The State is a function of society

To say that the State is one of the *functions of society* means that *State and society* cannot be separated, just as the lens of the retina couldn't be separated from the eye, or the eye would cease to be an eye. Even though the State is a special part of society, society cannot exist without the State. As an integral part of society, the State adopts the form of the capitalist society that it belongs to. Societal change translates into changes in the State and changes in the State presuppose changes in society. Hence, class struggle *shapes* each corner of society, as well as the State. For example, when the State approved the law for an eight-hour work day, it wasn't merely because there was a change within the *State*, but a change in *society as a whole*.

The law for an eight-hour workday—which undoubtedly went against the short-term interest of the capitalists—reflected the strengths that workers had against the dominant class. The State had to pass the eight-hour workday law to ensure the system's legitimacy, which was endangered by the growing momentum of anti-capitalist struggles.

The State derives from society

This is why the traditional Left was correct in their notion of the State, although for the wrong reasons. It is true that the State cannot be "neutral": it is *completely* capitalist to the degree that the society which the State corresponds to is also capitalist. The State does not have any grade of "autonomy" from society (not even relative autonomy). However, it is not true that the State is *only a tool* for the capitalists to use at their discretion. Class struggle can change important aspects of the State and its functions, to the same degree that resistance can change other aspects of society. The State *derives* from the society it belongs to, and from the way class struggle has shaped it.

THE STATE IS NOT A PERFECTLY DESIGNED MACHINE. STATE INSTITUTIONS, LEGISLATION, ETC, CHANGED DUE TO PRESSURES FROM THE SOCIAL STRUGGLES IN HISTORY. THE DIVERSE FORMS OF THE STATE APPARATUS CAN BE SEEN AS THE INSTITUTIONAL FOSSIL OF PAST STRUGGLES TO IMPOSE BOURGEOIS FORMS.

John Holloway (1947-)

A machine that divides and imposes hierarchies

The capitalist State is also a machine that *divides* people and imposes hierarchies. Firstly, it separates human beings into a multitude of different *political sovereignties*, or rather into nations ruled by separate States and divided by *borders*. As citizens we only have political rights within our own nation-states, and we lose those rights if we cross a border.

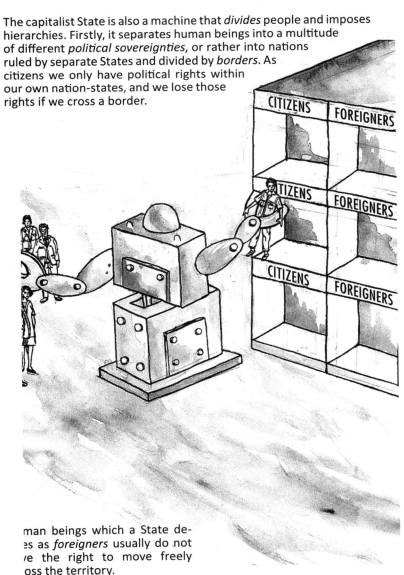

...man beings which a State de-
...es as *foreigners* usually do not
...ve the right to move freely
...oss the territory.

Global society, enclosed rights

Capitalism's own *nationalist ideology* makes us believe that the space for a society perfectly coincides with a State or nation. However, if we define society as a set of relationships that women and men establish among themselves and with nature, it's clear that these relationships are not limited to the borders of the country we live in.

EVEN THOUGH WE DON'T REALIZE IT, WE ARE ALL CONNECTED, FOR BETTER OR FOR WORSE. THE OPERATIONS OF PRODUCTION AND COMMERCE AND THE CIRCULATION OF IDEAS, TRENDS, FASHION, AND CULTURE CONNECT PEOPLE GLOBALLY.

There isn't a "French society" or a "Peruvian society," as if they were separate and independent entities. The society in which we live is global and interdependent.

States fragment, separate and divide global society, creating geographical zones, groups of privileged people and other oppressed groups. One of the major roles that the State plays is to limit our rights to the territory within closed borders, so that we can't change the way (global) society works.

Public and private

The second *separation* that the State has created exists between the *private* and the *public*. The legal and constitutional system establishes that there is an area of *life* that society can't "touch," because it is *private*. No one—not even the State—can enact laws over what is considered an individual's *private rights*. In principle, there isn't anything wrong with this. The problem is that under capitalism, only certain *types* of rights have this *privilege* of being considered *private* (or even considered *rights*).

WHY DOES THE LAW GUARANTEE REMUNERATION FOR ALL WORKERS, EXCEPT FOR THE WORK THAT WE WOMEN DO IN THE PRIVATE SPACE OF OUR HOMES?

WHY DOES THE STATE GUARANTEE PROTECTION OF PRIVATE PROPERTY, BUT NOT THE RIGHT TO HEALTH, EDUCATION, HOUSING AND WELL-BEING?

WHY CAN'T I TAKE A BUSINESSMAN'S PROPERTY, BUT HE CAN TAKE AWAY MY JOB?

WHY CAN'T WE DECIDE DEMOCRATICALLY HOW MUCH A PERSON CAN MAKE, OR WHAT TYPE OF ASSETS A PERSON CAN HOLD AS PROPERTY?

The line that separates a *right* from a mere *demand*, or *public* from *private*, is not set and has shifted throughout history. For centuries, men and women have struggled to bring *private privileges* back to the *public* sphere, so that society can democratically decide if they want to keep them or not.

But why don't we change things!?

WE LIVE IN A DEMOCRACY. IF PEOPLE REALLY WANTED TO CHANGE THINGS THEY COULD. AM I RIGHT?

Capitalism is an unjust social organization that causes enormous suffering for the majority of people: it produces poverty and exploitation, requires humans to be passive and limits their abilities, creates many forms of discrimination, feeds violence and fear, violates basic rights and pollutes the planet. Anti-capitalists have pointed this out for many years. Then, why don't we change things?

False democracy

Actually, we live in a *false democracy*. In the 19th century, when our ancestors began to fight for democracy, they referred to the original meaning of the word: *government by the people*. During this time, *liberal* elites firmly opposed the idea of democracy; liberalism has always been an enemy of democracy.

THE PEOPLE ARE NOT CAPABLE OF GOVERNING THEMSELVES. ONLY THE RICH AND PROPERTY OWNERS SHOULD HOLD POLITICAL RIGHTS SUCH AS VOTING. IF MOBS TAKE OVER GOVERNMENT, THERE WILL BE TYRANNY AND PRIVATE RIGHTS WILL BE ATTACKED.

After decades of struggle, the elites were forced to gradually grant rights such as the universal *right to vote*, regardless of one's social class. Liberals have since appropriated the word *democracy* as their own, but have radically changed the original meaning. Democracy no longer means "people's government"; instead it refers to an *electoral system* that decides which people will occupy State positions. Nothing more than that.

It is not a "people's government"

Today's democracy is in no way a government by the people. Representatives that we elect have very limited decision-making power. Their authority is limited to a *national territory* and to issues defined as *public*. Crucial aspects that affect our lives, such as the international flow of capital, for example, are completely out of our hands, because they take place in a global space. Democracy simply doesn't reach the *global realm*. Neither does it reach many of the things that national constitutions—inspired by *liberal* ideology—have defined as "*private* affairs."

If a pharmaceutical corporation, for example, patents a new drug that could save the lives of thousands, and the company decides to charge above the costs, at a price that most poor people can't afford, this is a *private* matter and the State can't intervene.

A dictatorship of capital

In addition, our democratic representatives have power over a very limited set of issues.

THE POWERFUL HAVE A WIDE RANGE OF CONTROL TO CONDITION POLITICAL DECISIONS THROUGH LEGAL MECHANISMS—SUCH AS ELECTION CAMPAIGN CONTRIBUTIONS AND MEDIA CONTROL—OR ILLEGAL MEANS SUCH AS BRIBES.

History has shown that democracy and political freedoms end once a representative or political party tries to go against the interests of the dominant class. A good example is the 1973 coup against democratically elected socialist president Salvador Allende in Chile, organized by the US government and local capitalists.

This is why we can't say that we live in a true democracy; really, we live in a dictatorship of capital in which we can choose representatives and make decisions regarding only minor issues.

Hegemony of the dominant class

The problem isn't only the lack of any real democracy. The dominant class not only controls through deceit and repression: most of its power derives from transforming its own *ideology* into the culture and "common sense" that we breathe on a daily basis.

THE DOMINANT CLASS ACHIEVES HEGEMONY WHEN IT IS ABLE TO WIN OVER THE MINDS AND HEARTS OF THE OPPRESSED. WHEN WE SPEAK IN THE LANGUAGE OF THE DOMINANT CLASS AND SEE THROUGH THEIR EYES, THAT'S WHEN HEGEMONY IS ACHIEVED.

Antonio Gramsci
(1891-1937)

DEAR ANTONIO, I WOULD ADD THAT THE DOMINANT CLASS'S POWER HAS PENETRATED EVEN OUR UNCONSCIOUS ACTIONS AND OUR BODIES.

Michel Foucault
(1926-1984)

I AGREE MICHEL, BUT LET'S NOT EXAGGERATE; THERE ALWAYS REMAINS A SPACE FOR RESISTANCE AND THE CONSTRUCTION OF A COUNTER-HEGEMONY.

Capitalism's ideology

Capitalism rests on its own *ideology*, or in other words, a structured set of ideas.

BUT AN IDEOLOGY ISN'T JUST THAT. FUNDAMENTALLY, IT IS A FORM OF FALSE CONSCIOUSNESS, A VISION THAT SUBTLY AND SILENTLY SENDS THE MESSAGE THAT SOCIETY CAN ONLY BE ORGANIZED BY THE DOMINANT CLASS.

LIBERALISM IS THE IDEOLOGY OF THE BOURGEOISIE.

Karl Marx

Liberalism holds that society is built by *individuals* and that these have certain *natural rights*. The rights of individuals have priority over the *sovereignty of the people*: no decision in society can go against these individual rights. On the contrary, society and the State should participate as little as possible, and not bother individuals. The State should only intervene when a law is violated or to provide minimum basic services. However, what makes liberalism an ideology isn't what it says, but *what it doesn't say*.

41

In theory, all human beings should be able to enjoy *natural rights*. But what liberals do not say is that these rights are *unevenly distributed*. *In theory*, one could have the right to a piece of land, but if this land is already *owned* by someone else, this right doesn't mean a thing. If someone is about to starve to death because other people have appropriated all the food, no law protects the *right to life*. The right of *freedom* means that one can do whatever he or she wishes without obstacles. But not everyone has the same opportunity to do whatever they want. And so: What does *freedom of press* mean when only a handful of people control the mass media?

REALLY, THERE ARE NO "NATURAL" RIGHTS. ALL RIGHTS HAVE BEEN DEFINED BY SOCIETY. THROUGHOUT HISTORY, WHEN LIBERALS SPEAK OF THE RIGHTS OF INDIVIDUALS, THEY ARE REALLY THINKING ONLY OF THE RIGHTS OF PROPRIETORS. THIS IS THE HEART OF BOURGEOIS IDEOLOGY.

Karl Marx

The culture of capitalism: individualism

The dominant class only reaches hegemony if it manages to transform its ideology into a mass culture, in the "common sense" of the majority of the population. Capitalism exists in part because it inhabits our minds and hearts: we breathe its culture every day.

The *individualism* of liberal ideology translates to a daily culture of egocentricity and isolation, which is characterized in the daily life of many people who shut themselves in their own private affairs.

Much of the *violence* and *fear* common in our societies comes from this egoism, and from the impulse *to be above others*. We keep our distance from others because we suppose that others can harm us for their own benefit. In a culture like this, it is difficult to develop relationships, solidarity, understanding and mutual caring.

Competitiveness, productivity, consumerism

The fact that a person can't enjoy many rights if they don't have economic resources is also reflected in a number of values in our culture. For example, productivity, the cult of economic success, competition and consumerism.

Many of the characteristics of our culture arise from our fear of not having sufficient resources to be "successful," along with the possibility of our using other people as tools for our own benefit. For example, our drive toward competitiveness and consumption results in disregard for the poor, racial discrimination and other forms of discrimination. In our culture, it is difficult for individuals to value traits such as love, friendship, camaraderie, creativity, etc.

Conformism and passivity

The liberal idea that there exists a "natural" order to things that shouldn't be questioned is reflected in *conformism, passivity* and the valuing of *obedience*, which are all examples of the characteristics we acquire during our education as children.

In order to survive, the capitalist system needs to assert values like selfishness, discrimination, and conformity *every day*. It accomplishes this through education and entertainment, advertising and the mass media. However, it is not a conspiracy to send a singular message. Capitalist culture is almost always disseminated in a spontaneous and unconscious form, not only because media, communication and entertainment are controlled by capitalists, but also because we have adopted this culture. We transmit capitalist culture in the words we use, the expectations that we have for our children, the objects that we consume, and in many other ways.

A total system?

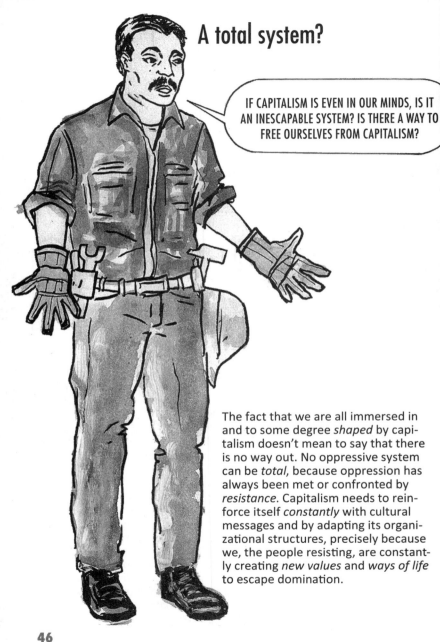

IF CAPITALISM IS EVEN IN OUR MINDS, IS IT AN INESCAPABLE SYSTEM? IS THERE A WAY TO FREE OURSELVES FROM CAPITALISM?

The fact that we are all immersed in and to some degree *shaped* by capitalism doesn't mean to say that there is no way out. No oppressive system can be *total*, because oppression has always been met or confronted by *resistance*. Capitalism needs to reinforce itself *constantly* with cultural messages and by adapting its organizational structures, precisely because we, the people resisting, are constantly creating *new values* and *ways of life* to escape domination.

From resistance to anti-capitalism

The most important *question* about capitalism we need to ask is how to transform our permanent resistance into a force capable of wiping out capitalism.

During its short history, anti-capitalism has explored various *answers*.

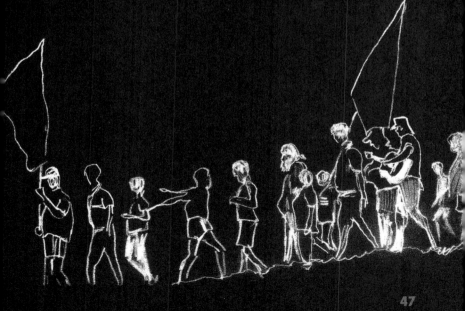

A little history

Anti-capitalism has both a short history and a long history. Even though it emerged less than 200 years ago, it inherited *long traditions* of past struggles that have nurtured ongoing resistance. We will begin with the "long history." *Resistance* is as old as oppression itself. The oppressed and exploited throughout the world have *resisted* long before capitalism surfaced, and in some of these struggles they created *new social forms*.

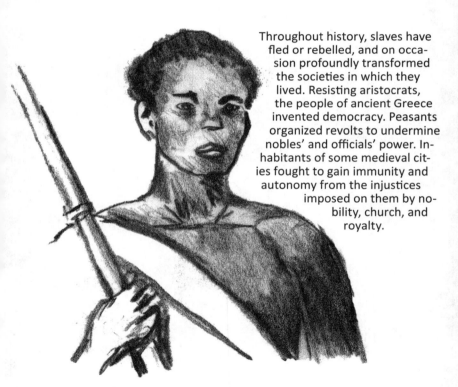

Throughout history, slaves have fled or rebelled, and on occasion profoundly transformed the societies in which they lived. Resisting aristocrats, the people of ancient Greece invented democracy. Peasants organized revolts to undermine nobles' and officials' power. Inhabitants of some medieval cities fought to gain immunity and autonomy from the injustices imposed on them by nobility, church, and royalty.

Through resistance, men and women gained new *rights* and discovered new ways to protect themselves against the powerful. As part of this resistance against oppression, they created new *myths* and *ideas*, or creatively reformulated previous ones.

Some people put them-selves at ease and imagined a world of happiness and respect that awaited them in another life, after they endured the pain and suffering of this world. Or they imagined a God that loves everyone equally, with-out social class distinctions.

Later, some medieval peasant movements believed that the kingdom of love would not only await them in another world, but would soon arrive on earth for the living by the grace of God.

These ideas helped the oppressed keep their optimism and continue to re-sist, but they also helped people to begin to think about how they wanted to live. Each new generation used these myths and ideas, and transformed them according to their imagination and the needs of the struggles.

49

The "revolution" of humanism

A very important cultural transformation took place in Europe between the 13th and 16th century, a change that would help catapult resistance in new directions. At this time, most people believed that only *transcendental* forces (God) controlled what happened on earth. If the world was the way it was, it was because of *divine intervention*, which the human mind had no way to perceive. Naturally, this belief helped to affirm the power of priests, nobility and royalty, which declared that God's will determined each person's social position. However, even those who resisted power believed that change would come from the *transcendental* realm, from divine will. At this time, some thinkers began to apprehensively suggest the notion that this world *belonged to human beings*. By using the ability to reason, men and women could understand the world, transform it, and *decide* their own fates.

IN THE MIDST OF THE ARTISTIC AND SCIENTIFIC RENAISSANCE, HUMAN BEINGS DECLARED THEMSELVES MASTERS OVER THEIR OWN LIVES.

IN THOSE ORIGINS OF MODERNITY, KNOWLEDGE SHIFTED FROM THE TRANSCENDENTAL PLANE TO THE IMMANENT, AND CONSEQUENTLY HUMAN KNOWLEDGE BECAME A DOING, A PRACTICE OF TRANSFORMING NATURE. THIS CHANGE WAS A FUNDAMENTAL CHANGE IN CULTURE: IT WAS A REVOLUTION.

Antonio Negri (1933-)

As God became a more distant presence, human beings gained confidence in themselves, in their own capacity to *create* and *decide*. The *political* implications of this conceptual revolution didn't take long to become visible.

Marsilio
de Padua
(1275?-1342)

THE POWER OF THE REPUBLIC AND THE POWER OF ITS LAWS DO NOT DERIVE FROM SUPERIOR PRINCIPLES, BUT FROM THE BODY OF CITIZENS.

QUIET, HERETIC!

WHAT WILL WE DO IF THE PEOPLE BEGIN TO BELIEVE THEY CAN DECIDE FOR THEMSELVES?

DON'T WORRY, THE PEOPLE CAN'T READ.

MARSILIO DE PADUA THE DEFENDER OF PEACE

Since then, many other thinkers tried to reinforce *obedience* through supposed principles of "rationality" and "science." However, the damage was already done: since then, more men and women slowly liberated their minds and imagined that *they could create* a different world. The invention of the printing press in 1440 and the capacity to travel longer distances improved communication and the circulation of ideas and dreams among people from different places and social groups.

Rebels, utopians, enlightened, and romantics

Meanwhile, the development of capitalism introduced new forms of oppression for Europeans and also for the other peoples that the system began to colonize. Resistance intensified, and along with the struggles came the need to imagine a better world. From the 16th century onward, significant revolts and revolutions took place, always accompanied by new efforts to imagine a different world.

The German peasants who joined Thomas Müntzer in his great revolt of the beginning of that century, for example, found inspiration in biblical stories. Müntzer's peasants organized themselves into a sect and decided to collectivize property, so as to live life just as they imagined the early Christians had done. They were defeated, but the memory of his revolt was passed down from generation to generation.

Thomas Müntzer
(1489?-1525)

Others found inspiration in the *utopias* written by authors such as Tomás Moro in 1516, Campanella in 1602, and many others. These thinkers described how imaginary cities would function, inhabited by citizens who would live in equality, without property or money. Other writers, who traveled abroad, gave accounts of societies in faraway lands, where entire people lived as equals and free from oppression.

In the 18th century, philosophers of the *Enlightenment* chose to rely on their own capacity for reason. They designed *reforms* for society, or completely new *social systems*.

History offered many more sources of inspiration for how to build a better world. Ancient Athenian democracy ignited the imagination of many. Others, like the 19th century *Romantics*, were inspired by medieval life, which for them was free of the oppression of money and the horrific spectacle of the modern factories and pollution.

All of these histories, myths, and ideas circulated around the world and among classes, in a long process of building a *collective imagination* for a better world. The series of *revolutions* that began in Europe in the mid 17th century created the perfect breeding ground for this collective process. The resistance fed dreams of a different world, and at the same time inspired new struggles for emancipation.

A revolutionary tradition is born: the English Revolution

In 1648, a revolution overthrew and decapitated Charles I, King of England, and in the following years the country functioned as a Republic. Even though it began as a conflict among elites, soon the "common people" joined the revolution. Peasants, artisans and city laborers, the "men with no master" who lived in the public forests and land that remained, had good motives for discontent. The revolution led to fervent political debates and many dared to question the different forms of oppression and demanded radical changes.

The most radical were finally defeated, but after the revolution, the monarchy and nobility were never the same. The radicals' message remained, and the future revolutions used their ideals of freedom and equality.

The French Revolution

Other revolutions followed the one of 1648. During the 1770s there was a chain reaction of revolts and revolutions in many countries. However, it was the French Revolution of 1789 that sparked the desperate cries for emancipation among men and women throughout the world. In 18th century France there was a climate of intense debate over new ideas, known as the *Enlightenment*.

Jean-Jacques Rousseau (1712-1778)

MEN LIVED IN AN IDEAL STATE UNTIL PRIVATE PROPERTY BROUGHT INEQUALITY AND ALONG WITH IT MUCH OF THE PRESENT SUFFERING.

DISCOURSE ON THE ORIGIN OF INEQUALITY

Denis Diderot (1713-1784)

SLAVERY AND THE COLONIES ARE A DISGRACE THAT EUROPE CANNOT PERMIT!

KINGS TURN INTO TYRANTS TOO EASILY. WOULDN'T A DEMOCRACY BE BETTER?

The revolution started as a protest of nobles against the King's injustices, but that soon provoked the participation of other social groups: merchants, professionals, peasants, urban poor, and artisans.

The Revolution placed limits on the King's power with a constitution that guaranteed *rights to men* and eliminated some of the most irritating feudal privileges. This didn't satisfy the masses' desire for change.

The most radicalized revolutionaries—the Jacobins—knew how to win the support of the poor. In 1793, Louis XVI was executed by guillotine. The Jacobins declared *popular sovereignty*, in what was one of the first experiences of modern democracy. A *reaction* didn't take long to arrive, and in 1794 the Jacobins were replaced by a more moderate sector. However, many of the changes that the Revolution produced were irreversible. The idea of a *popular government*, the presence of the *masses* in political life and the desire for *equality* were to remain.

Echoes of the Revolution: antiracism, national self-determination, and feminism

The French Revolution ignited the imagination of men and women around the planet. Some of the changes in France rapidly expanded to other countries. The message of the Revolution also encouraged the fight for emancipation in the *New World*. Many broadened their aspirations of freedom, equality, and fraternity in relation to *race*, *nations,* and *gender*.

For example, in 1804, people of African ancestry in the French colony of Santo Domingo (today Haiti) declared themselves *independent*.

Capitalism had uprooted them from Africa to work in plantations. Africans in the colonies resisted oppression in thousands of ways. The revolution in 1789 inspired enslaved Africans to fight for emancipation and equality.

Touissaint L'Ouverture (1743-1803) leader of African and Afro-Haitian rebels.

ONLY BECAUSE WE ARE BLACK WE CANNOT HAVE THE FREEDOM, EQUALITY, AND FRATERNITY YOU HAVE DECLARED IN FRANCE?

Touissaint was captured and died in France in 1803. However, the struggle for emancipation of minorities and race equality would become an unstoppable force, along with the aspiration for *national liberation* in many of the colonial countries. The ideals of freedom and equality moved to the relations between *nations*, with many colonial countries declaring the right to decide their own destiny.

Women also felt that the slogan of freedom, equality, and fraternity spoke to their needs and that these newly accepted *rights* shouldn't be a privilege for only *men*.

WOMEN SHOULD HAVE THE SAME EQUAL RIGHTS AS MEN, IN THEIR PRIVATE LIVES AS WELL IN PUBLIC LIFE. WE WANT THE RIGHT TO VOTE, AND TO ELECT OUR REPRESENTATIVES. WE WANT ACCESS TO EDUCATION AND PROPERTY. WE WANT FREEDOM!

Olympe de Gouges
(1748-1793)

Although she was sent to the guillotine in 1793, the legacy of Olympe de Gouges inspired women to continue to fight for their rights. Her *Declaration of the Rights of Woman and the Female Citizen* became a key text in the development of a feminist movement.

The Industrial Revolution: rise of the proletariat

Meanwhile, in Europe, capitalism had radically changed the organization of production. The *Industrial Revolution* dramatically changed the lives of workers and converted new segments of the population into the *proletariat*.

Thousands of artisans and peasants were displaced from their lands and forced to work in the new factories. Men, women, and children worked fourteen-hour workdays, sometimes longer, for miserable wages and in unsafe working conditions. The smoke and waste from the factories polluted the water and air, especially in areas populated by the poor.

Slowly, workers began to organize. They established *mutual associations* and *trade unions* and held *strikes* for better working conditions. Many felt it was necessary to imagine a *new society* free from the miseries of capitalism. As part of their daily *struggles*, the workers discovered the long legacy of the *collective imagination* of a new world that past struggles brought into light. Through their *experience* and *creativity*, they recreated this legacy and added new elements.

The birth of the Socialist tradition

Here is where we'll begin anti-capitalism's "short history."
Even though *socialism* was founded around 1830,
it was nurtured by previous struggles and
dreams for emancipation.

IT WAS AN EFFERVESCENT TIME IN
EUROPE. WORKER MOBILIZATIONS
GREW, ALONG WITH THE STRUGGLE
FOR UNIVERSAL SUFFRAGE, AND IN SOME
COUNTRIES THE FIGHT FOR NATIONAL
SELF-DETERMINATION. REVOLUTION WAS
IN THE AIR.

Socialism was born in this context, and it was the first specifically *anti-capitalist* movement. Socialists identified capitalism as the *cause* for many of the wrongdoings in society, and they began to imagine how to create and organize a new world free from all forms of oppression.

At first, *socialism* was mostly a fluid and widespread movement. It didn't have parties, programs or well defined ideas; it didn't even have a specific name. It could be called indistinctly "socialism," "mutualism," "communism," "associationism," "cooperativism," among others.

WE CAN ORGANIZE PRODUCTION IN A MORE HUMANE AND COOPERATIVE STRUCTURE IF WE CHANGE THIS INDIVIDUALISTIC AND COMPETITIVE INDUSTRIALISM. I AM GOING TO CREATE MODEL COMMUNITIES AND FACTORIES, TO PROVE THAT MEN CAN LIVE IN MUTUAL HARMONY.

NEW MORAL WORLD

Robert Owen (1771-1858)

INDUSTRIAL LABOR DEGRADES HUMAN BEINGS. I WILL SET UP COMMUNITIES OR "PHALANSTARIES," WHERE PRIVATE PROPERTY WILL BE COLLECTIVIZED, WHERE WOMEN WILL HAVE THE SAME RIGHTS AS MEN, AND SEXUAL FREEDOM WILL BE A RIGHT FOR EVERYONE.

Charles Fourier (1772-1837)

Even though socialism is thought of as a *working class* movement, throughout its history a diverse array of social groups participated in it. Because it proposes to end *all forms of oppression*, socialism attracted the poor and workers, but also students, artists, small merchants and producers. More recently, socialism attracted national minorities and the racially oppressed, indigenous peoples and environmentalists, and everyone affected by capitalism.

Anarchism

During the second half of the 19th century, more clearly defined ideologies began to develop *within* the socialist movement. *Anarchism as a school of thought* set itself apart by opposing all forms of oppression (and not just *economic* exploitation) and by rejecting the State and centralized authority. Anarchists criticized communists and other socialists for advocating ideas like the "dictatorship of the proletariat" and "State socialism," which they considered authoritarian.

ONCE WORKERS CONTROL THE ECONOMY, THE FUNCTIONS OF THE STATE WILL BE REABSORBED IN SOCIETY. WE WILL ORGANIZE SOCIETY INTO A DECENTRALIZED FEDERATION OF FREE PRODUCERS, WITHOUT A STATE.

The father of anarchism, Pierre-Joseph Proudhon, believed that the economy had to be progressively modified so that workers could gain control over production. Even though he believed that "property was theft," he sustained that all people should be *small owners* of the means of production.

WHAT IS PROPERTY?

Pierre-Joseph
Proudhon (1809-1865)

Differing from other socialists, anarchists believed that the forms of organizing the struggle against capitalism should reflect non-hierarchical and federative principles. This is why they avoided forming political *parties*, although they supported *syndical* organization. On the other hand, there were many differences among anarchists surrounding violence, clandestine actions and armed cells.

Piotr Kropotkin
(1842-1921)

WE SHOULD FREE OURSELVES FROM AUTHORITY, THE STATE, GOD AND PROPERTY. THE STATE DIVIDES AND OPPRESSES PEOPLE. IT GOES AGAINST SOCIETY AND THIS IS WHY IT SHOULD BE DESTROYED.

THE CONQUEST OF BREAD

Mikhail Bakunin

I AGREE MIKHAIL, BUT I DON'T LIKE YOUR INSURRECTIONAL AND VIOLENT TACTICS. WE NEED TO DEVELOP COOPERATION AND MUTUAL AID.

STATISM AND ANARCHY

Anarchism influenced labor movements in many parts of the world during the 19th and early 20th century, especially in Europe and the Americas. Eventually, its importance declined considerably.

Marxism

Within the socialist tradition, Marxism—the school of thought inspired by German philosopher Karl Marx—gained many supporters.

> CAPITALISM SUPPOSES A CONTINUOUS CLASS STRUGGLE BETWEEN THE BOURGEOISIE AND THE PROLETARIAT OR WORKING CLASS. THIS HISTORICAL AGENT IS DESTINED TO DEFEAT CAPITALISM AND EMANCIPATE SOCIETY.

Different from anarchism, Marxism argued that the State should be used as a key *tool* for changing society. To *take power*, communists should organize themselves in centralized parties, which could make it to government. A period of a *dictatorship of the proletariat* is needed to impose changes. Then, once classes have been eliminated and property over the means of production *collectivized*, the absence of oppression would make the State unnecessary. In a *communist* society, the State would disappear along with inequality.

Marx dedicated most of his writing to a critique of capitalism, and wrote very little about what a future society would look like, or how to organize resistance against the system. However, there is a lot of debate over how much of what we call *Marxism* is based on the *true* ideas of Marx. One thing is clear: Friedrich Engels contributed to creating a distorted image of the ideas of his great friend, by presenting them as a *scientific* and *flawless* doctrine capable of explaining all social phenomena and to even predict the future.

MARX IS THE NEWTON OF SOCIAL SCIENCES; HIS SOCIALISM IS THE ONLY SCIENTIFIC TRUTH. THE REST IS NOTHING BUT UTOPIAN SOCIALISM.

I DIDN'T SAY THAT.

KARL MARX
1818-1883

Friedrich Engels (1820-1895)

Marxism was a fundamental tool for understanding how capitalism functions and for dreaming a new world. During the second half of the 19th century and most of the 20th century, Marxism inspired millions to fight for socialism. However, by converting itself into a *dogma*, it was difficult for Marxist socialism to make room for diverse political tactics and to adapt itself to different situations and historical changes.

First International

In 1864, the first *International Workingmen's Association,* known as the *First International,* was organized. Delegates from worker movements from different countries came together for the event. The aim was the co-ordination of workers' struggles to end capitalism throughout the world. Marx himself, a delegate of German workers, took charge of writing the statutes and had a central role in forming the new organization. However, some anarchists opposed Marx's ideas; Bakunin precipitated the crisis by calling on workers to create an "antiauthoritarian" *International.*

Mikhail Bakunin

Karl Marx

After several disputes, Marx gained support to expulse Bakunin from the *International* in 1872. Since then, the *International* declined until it finally broke up in 1876. Despite its short life, the *First International* was very important in the development of socialism and internationalism in many parts of the world.

The first socialist parties

When Marx and Engels wrote the *Communist Manifesto* (1848), the word *party* had a different meaning than it does today. They didn't refer to a particular *organization*, but a *wide range* of ideas and interests that would naturally appear to the exploited. The first socialist parties as they are *currently* understood—that's to say, a centralized *organization*, directed by enlightened *leaders* and endowed with a *program*—first appeared in Germany in the 1860s. The *social democratic* parties—as they were called—identified with *Marxist* ideas.

WORKERS CANNOT ACHIEVE SOCIALIST CONSCIOUSNESS BY THEMSELVES: ON THE CONTRARY, IT MUST BE BROUGHT TO THEM FROM OUTSIDE SOURCES. SOCIALISM IS A SCIENCE THAT PARTY INTELLECTUALS SHOULD TEACH TO WORKERS.

THE ROLE OF THE PARTY IS TO EDUCATE THE PROLETARIAT, TO SUPPLY THEM WITH CONSCIOUSNESS OF THEIR SITUATION AND THEIR TASK.

Karl Kautsky (1854-1938)
Social democratic leader

German social democracy's initial success drove worker movements throughout Europe and other continents to emulate the party model.

In 1889, the Second International was created, homogenized by the German socialists. Before World War I, socialist parties were founded in Austria, Scandinavia, Russia, Holland, Belgium, the United States, Italy, France, Spain, England, Australia, Poland, Bulgaria, Hungary, Chile, Argentina, Japan, Canada, China, Brazil, and other places.

67

Reform or revolution?
Social Democracy splits up

Between 1890 and 1914, a deep debate among Marxists unleashed, which ended in a divide within Marxism. German social democrats noted a certain contradiction between a political *practice* increasingly centered on "legal" work in parliament, and a *theory* that continued to advocate revolution. This is why Eduard Bernstein, one of social democracy's most important leaders, embarked on a critical *revision* of Marx's ideas. He wanted to free the Party from the revolutionary theory, so to attain more votes, not only from workers, but also from other social groups. His *revisionism* sparked a bitter debate with the *communist* or *revolutionary socialists*.

WE CAN'T WAIT FOR CAPITALISM TO UNDERGO REFORMATION ON ITS OWN. WE HAVE TO TAKE ADVANTAGE OF THE LEGAL MECHANISMS THAT DEMOCRACY OFFERS TO BEGIN TO INTRODUCE GRADUAL REFORMS IN THE ECONOMIC AND POLITICAL SYSTEMS.

THIS IS WHY IT IS BEST TO GAIN THE SUPPORT OF THE MIDDLE SECTORS OF THE POPULATION, NOT JUST THE WORKERS. BY GRADUALLY PENETRATING DEMOCRACY, WE CAN IMPROVE CONDITIONS FOR WORKERS AND REACH SOCIALISM.

Eduard Bernstein
(1850-1932)

EDUARD, YOUR REFORMISM IS ONLY PETIT-BOURGEOIS OPPORTUNISM. IT ISN'T THAT IT'S BAD TO MAKE REFORMS THAT WOULD IMPROVE WORKERS' LIVES. BUT ANY GRADUAL REFORM PROGRAM WITHIN THE STATE WILL BE LIMITED BY CAPITALIST INTERESTS. WE CANNOT ACHIEVE SOCIALISM WITHOUT A REVOLUTION, AND I DON'T THINK THAT WORKERS SHOULD MAKE COMPROMISES WITH OTHER CLASSES.

Eduard Bernstein

Rosa Luxemburg (1871-1919), revolutionary leader

The divide between *communists* and *reformists* grew even deeper during World War I. In 1914, most socialist representatives in several countries decided to support their states in entering the war. This meant sending workers to fight against other workers and a betrayal of one of the most important traditions within socialism: *internationalism*. Communism regrouped along the margins of social democracy, and in 1921, the *German Social Democratic Party* formally adopted Bernstein's *revisionist* ideas. Most socialist parties throughout the world adopted similar politics, and soon *social democracy* became synonymous with *reformism*. The divide between *reformists* and *revolutionaries* was sealed.

69

The Russian Revolution: the first anti-capitalist revolution

In the first three decades of the 20th century, a wave of anti-capitalist struggles shook many parts of the world.

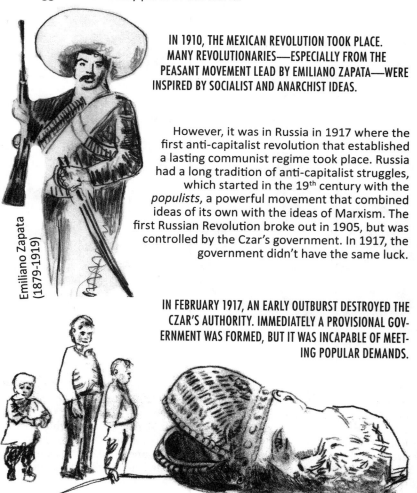

IN 1910, THE MEXICAN REVOLUTION TOOK PLACE. MANY REVOLUTIONARIES—ESPECIALLY FROM THE PEASANT MOVEMENT LEAD BY EMILIANO ZAPATA—WERE INSPIRED BY SOCIALIST AND ANARCHIST IDEAS.

However, it was in Russia in 1917 where the first anti-capitalist revolution that established a lasting communist regime took place. Russia had a long tradition of anti-capitalist struggles, which started in the 19th century with the *populists*, a powerful movement that combined ideas of its own with the ideas of Marxism. The first Russian Revolution broke out in 1905, but was controlled by the Czar's government. In 1917, the government didn't have the same luck.

Emiliano Zapata (1879-1919)

IN FEBRUARY 1917, AN EARLY OUTBURST DESTROYED THE CZAR'S AUTHORITY. IMMEDIATELY A PROVISIONAL GOVERNMENT WAS FORMED, BUT IT WAS INCAPABLE OF MEETING POPULAR DEMANDS.

Workers then began to occupy their workplaces, demanding *workers' control* over production. Peasants occupied land from landowners. Soldiers refused to follow superiors' orders. The national minorities rejected the authority of the Russian imperial State. Many students and artists joined the struggle, as well as feminists.

> Everywhere, men and women declared themselves masters over their own destinies and refused to take orders. In October 1917, power collapsed.

In Russia, revolutionaries followed different schools of thought. Some advocated *federative* principles from anarchism. Others joined different *parties* that existed. *Unions* also had an important role.

HOWEVER, THE SOVIETS WERE THE MOST IMPORTANT INSTITUTION THAT WOULD EMERGE FROM THE RUSSIAN REVOLUTION. THE SOVIETS WERE COUNCILS IN WHICH WORKERS, PEASANTS, SOLDIERS AND OTHER GROUPS PARTICIPATED. THROUGH DEBATE AND DEMOCRATIC STRUCTURE, THESE COUNCILS MADE THE MOST IMPORTANT DECISIONS DURING THE REVOLUTION AND AFTERWARD.

Bolsheviks in government

From February to October, 1917, the *Bolshevik* Party, then a relatively small political force, gained support from the majority of sectors struggling for revolution.

After the armed insurrection of October 24-25, 1917, the Soviet of Petrograd named Vladimir Lenin, a prominent Bolshevik leader, the president of the "Council of People's Commissars"—that was how the new Soviet government was called.

Vladimir Lenin (1870-1924)

With the new regime, the revolution made a series of radical measures in the creation of a communist society. The government expropriated land from the church and large landowners, nationalized industry, and ceased privileges for nobility and the bourgeoisie. National minorities received a much more egalitarian treatment, and women acquired new rights. In 1922, the Union of Soviet Socialist Republics (USSR) was founded to become the first experiment in a communist society in history.

Leninism

In 1903, Lenin began to develop a new concept about party organization. Like Kautsky, the Bolshevik leader advocated that intellectuals introduce workers "from the outside," a communist *consciousness* that workers could never develop alone.

LENIN
WHAT IS TO BE DONE?

UNDERSTOOD.

THE PARTY IS THE VANGUARD THAT LEADS THE PROLETARIAT. WE NEED A STRONGLY CENTRALIZED PARTY OF PROFESSIONAL REVOLUTIONARIES, DIRECTED BY A HANDFUL OF "STRONG MINDS." ONLY WORKERS WITH A HIGHLY DEVELOPED CLASS CONSCIOUSNESS WILL BE ABLE TO JOIN THE PARTY. AND THOSE WHO DEPARTED FROM THE PARTY PROGRAM WILL BE EXPULSED.

In the "democratic centralism" that Lenin imagined, the Party bases would have the right to choose their *leaders*, albeit *indirectly*. But then, all members would have to accept the party line that they "imposed."

After the Russian Revolution, the Bolsheviks gained prestige worldwide. In 1919, Lenin organized the Third International that would link revolutionaries from around the world. Almost everywhere, communists copied the Leninist party model and the political line of the Bolsheviks.

Heirs to Leninism: Stalinism and Trotskyism

After the 1930s, several ideologies were claimed to be heirs to "Marxist-Leninism": *Stalinism, Trotskyism, Maoism,* and *Guevarism. Stalinism* and *Trotskyism* arose from the confrontations between Bolshevik leaders following the death of Lenin, in 1924. *Joseph Stalin* (1878-1953) gained power, annihilating all his possible rivals. *Leon Trotsky,* Lenin's old comrade, was expelled from his position and forced into exile, from which he harshly criticized the *Soviet political regime* (even though he never ceased to defend the *social* and *economic* structures the regime had helped to build).

THE USSR IS A WORKERS' STATE, BUT TODAY IT IS DECLINING BECAUSE OF ITS BUREAUCRATIC POLITICAL REGIME.

SOCIALISM MUST BE A WORLD SYSTEM: IT CAN'T EXIST IN "ONLY ONE COUNTRY" AS STALIN SAYS.

TROTSKY
REVOLUTION
BETRAYED

Leon Trotsky
(1879-1940)

Before he was murdered by an agent of Stalin, Trotsky tried to form the *Fourth International* in 1938, to reorganize the communist movement around his ideas. But his efforts failed: *Stalinism* continued to prevail as the predominant communist school of thought in the world. Trotskyism, weakened by its own permanent internal disputes, never became a true movement of masses.

Maoism

Maoism formed in the 1960s, grouping together followers of Mao Zedong, leader of the 1949 Chinese Revolution. Like Trotskyists, Maoists were clustered in opposition to the Soviet leadership and the hegemony of Stalinism. Followers were drawn to Maoism due to the strong anti-bureaucratic beliefs that Mao had sometimes advocated, and to his re-evaluation of the revolutionary role of the peasantry.

IN A COUNTRY LIKE CHINA, THE PEASANTRY IS THE MAIN ALLY OF COMMUNISTS. IF WE HAD FOLLOWED THE SOVIET DOGMA, WE WOULD HAVE ONLY BEEN SUPPORTED BY THE WORKERS, AND WE NEVER WOULD HAVE BEEN ABLE TO START THE CHINESE REVOLUTION.

MAO ZEDONG THE RED BOOK

Mao Zedong
(1893-1976)

The Maoists rejected Stalinism's emphasis on the exclusive role of the working class: the peasantry was called upon to take a central position in the direction of world revolution. Maoists also believed that the main international conflict wasn't between the bourgeoisie and the proletariat, but between capitalist nations and the underdeveloped nations. Another distinctive trait of Maoists is their particularly strong confidence that *willpower* was the only requisite for important social and mental changes.

Guevarism

In Latin America, during the 1960s, a school of thought loosely related to Leninism emerged, which differentiated itself by the centrality it granted to *guerilla warfare*. *Guevarism* or *Foquismo* advocated organizing small armed groups that would open an insurrectional guerilla "focus" in peasant areas.

IF WE CAN OPEN AN INITIAL FOCUS, OUR POWER WILL GROW THANKS TO THE SUPPORT OF THE POPULATION THAT WE ARE LIBERATING, UNTIL WE LIBERATE THE ENTIRE COUNTRY.

BOLIVIA

Che Guevara
(1928-1967)

In this theory, the idea of the *vanguard* is taken to the extreme. Emancipation becomes the task of a handful of guerilla soldiers with special training, while the role of the oppressed remains blurry.

Historically, the different Leninist schools of thought have clashed; however, they also have many commonalities. They all emphasize the need *to take power* though a *vanguard* party/army that is strongly *centralized*. They also agree upon what future society should look like: nationalized means of production, the maintenance of a one-party regime, and centralized planning of the economy.

National Liberation Movements

There are other types of movements that sometimes consider themselves anti-capitalist. In countries dominated by colonialism, the struggle for *national sovereignty* and against *developed empires* (that's to say, capitalists) is often presented as *socialist*. National Liberation Movements (NLM) tended to combine *socialism* and *nationalism* in varying proportions. Some ideas from Marxism have attracted national liberation movements: the role of the Party, nationalized economy, and, to some degree, equality. Other ideas, such as class struggle, tended to be avoided, in order to mobilize not only workers and peasants, but also sectors of the "national bourgeoisie."

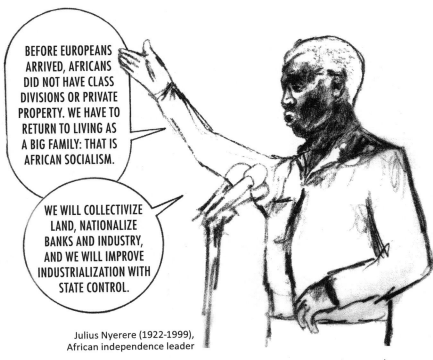

BEFORE EUROPEANS ARRIVED, AFRICANS DID NOT HAVE CLASS DIVISIONS OR PRIVATE PROPERTY. WE HAVE TO RETURN TO LIVING AS A BIG FAMILY: THAT IS AFRICAN SOCIALISM.

WE WILL COLLECTIVIZE LAND, NATIONALIZE BANKS AND INDUSTRY, AND WE WILL IMPROVE INDUSTRIALIZATION WITH STATE CONTROL.

Julius Nyerere (1922-1999),
African independence leader

The example of rapid industrialization in the USSR attracted a number of Third World movements to follow the communist example. In many cases, leaders used socialism as an *ideology* that helped to *concentrate* power for purposes of *economic development*, rather than the *emancipation of* the people.

Failure of the Communist project

The three great movements rooted in the socialist tradition—*communism*, *social democracy* and the *National Libration Movement*—had the opportunity to implement programs in several countries. For different reasons, all three failed.

The expectations that Russia's *communist project* generated soon became frustrated. Using the emergency situation as an excuse, the new government began to renounce the achievements of the Revolution.

I PROHIBIT THE CONSTITUENT ASSEMBLY TO MEET FROM NOW ON. ONLY THE COMMUNIST PARTY CAN EXIST, AND WITHIN OUR PARTY THERE CAN'T BE INTERNAL FRACTIONS OR DISSIDENCE.

THE SOVIETS WILL BE ABLE TO CONTINUE TO FUNCTION: ANYWAY, REAL POWER IS ALREADY IN THE HANDS OF THE PARTY. WORKERS' CONTROL OVER PRODUCTION SHOULD CEASE BECAUSE OF ITS INEFFICIENCY. IN ITS PLACE, WE THE STATE WILL NAME COMPANY DIRECTORS.

Vladimir Lenin

Leon Trotsky

Many sexual, artistic, union and press freedoms were curtailed. In his ascent to power, Stalin drastically worsened conditions. Beginning in 1928, thousands of "suspicious" people were condemned to death or sent to concentration camps. Many of the peasants were forced to collectivize their lands, and the State imposed terrible disciplinary measures against workers and the general population. Non-Russian nationalities returned to an oppressive situation.

The USSR made surprising improvements in the economy, education and health for the soviet people. However, exploitation and oppression did not disappear, but were simply replaced by new forms.

LENIN'S PARTY ENDED UP IMPOSING ON SOCIETY ITS OWN CENTRALIZED AND HIERARCHICAL STRUCTURES. THE BUREAUCRACY REPLACED THE CAPITALISTS AS THE NEW DOMINANT CLASS, WHICH EXPLOITED WORKERS THROUGH ITS CONTROL OVER POLITICAL AND ECONOMIC DECISIONS.

Other countries implemented the communist model. In all cases, it produced similar results, far from the ideals of equality and emancipation. In the 1980s, the USSR entered a severe economic crisis. The USSR's bureaucrats abandoned communism, tempted by the notions of personal wealth and becoming bourgeois. The Soviet government began to adopt neoliberal policies. After 1989, most communist countries followed capitalism's path. In 1991, when the USSR collapsed, the historic failure of communism not only left anti-capitalist with an enormous political defeat, but also a moral defeat.

Failure of the social democratic project

The *reformist* project also had an opportunity to be put into practice. During the 20th century, social democratic parties won power in many European countries. Governments passed wide-reaching social *reform* programs to improve workers' lives and those of the most vulnerable sectors of society.

FROM WITHIN GOVERNMENT WE WILL CREATE A "WELFARE STATE." WE WILL USE PUBLIC FUNDS TO FINANCE HOUSING, HEALTH PROGRAMS, ASSISTANCE FOR SINGLE MOTHERS, FREE PUBLIC EDUCATION, PENSIONS, AND UNEMPLOYMENT FUNDS.

Olof Palme (1927-1986)
Social democratic Prime Minister of Sweden

Welfare policies undoubtedly improved the lives of workers, but they did not contribute to ending exploitation and oppression. They only slightly improved the most severe *effects* of exploitation and oppression. This is why some think that reformist policies have perfected capitalism, rather than bringing society closer to socialism, converting the State into an even more effective apparatus of control.

Subsequently, even the most moderate reforms began to dismantle in most countries. In the 1980s many social democratic governments led the dismantling themselves. In its efforts to reach socialism through *gradual reforms* within the State, the social democratic program failed.

The failure of the national liberation project

The NLMs had some success in displacing traditional elites from many Third World countries, and in some cases were able to carry out ambitious industrialization programs. However, they did not make real progress in implementing truly emancipatory or anti-capitalist measures. In addition, they couldn't break with economic dependency and imperialism. On the contrary, often the new elites that tried to replace traditional elites used a nationalist, pseudo-egalitarian, statist discourse to submit the population to greater exploitation for the sake of "development." In the 1980s and 1990s, most *national liberation* governments lost power and embraced the neoliberal model.

DREAMS HAVE ENDED. IT IS 1985; TIMES HAVE CHANGED. THE ECONOMY IS IN CRISIS AND WE NEED INVESTMENTS. IT'S TIME TO PRIVATIZE THE ECONOMY AND TO MAKE AMENDS WITH EUROPE.

Julius Nyerere

Neoliberalism's advance and the "end of history"

As all of its rivals were failing, capitalism seemed to gain unstoppable momentum. Even in the wealthiest nations, the welfare state began to fall apart, and workers lost their rights.

Ronald Reagan (1911-2004)

Margaret Thatcher (1925-)

> WE ARE IN THE ERA OF GLOBALIZATION; IT IS TIME TO PRIVATIZE, SHRINK THE GOVERNMENT, AND FREE UP MARKETS. BANKS AND BIG BUSINESSES SHOULD HAVE ABSOLUTE FREEDOM TO CONDUCT BUSINESS AND MOVE CAPITAL THROUGHOUT THE WORLD WITHOUT RESTRICTIONS.

Neo-liberalism had become the "single thought" and no one seemed to have any viable alternative. Men and women's sorrow over the loss of hope for emancipation was countered by capitalist euphoria.

> THIS IS THE "END OF HISTORY": THE WORLD IS NOT GOING TO CHANGE BECAUSE THERE IS NO BETTER OPTION THAN CAPITALISM. CRITICS ARE JUST NOSTALGIC.

Francis Fukuyama (1952-), North American government advisor

The rise of a new anti-capitalism

Meanwhile, capitalism's rapid advance deeply affected the majority of people on earth.

Unemployment and flexible labor standards hit workers around the world, especially women. Commercial occupation of lands and forests and the development of genetically modified foods ruined consumers and farmers, and particularly indigenous people. Neoliberal reforms and foreign debt suffocated the Third World. Capital speculation produced frequent financial crises. Corporate control of mass media threatened freedom of expression and political rights.

Repression and institutional racism grows, and jails have been filled with the poor and ethnic minorities. War has spread throughout the globe to punish nations that could potentially threaten the interests of the capitalist empire. Health, safety, and education have become privileges for the few. The rapid deterioration of the environment puts the future of humanity at risk.

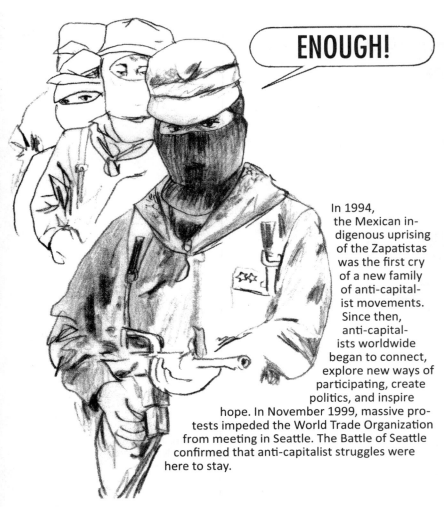

ENOUGH!

In 1994, the Mexican indigenous uprising of the Zapatistas was the first cry of a new family of anti-capitalist movements. Since then, anti-capitalists worldwide began to connect, explore new ways of participating, create politics, and inspire hope. In November 1999, massive protests impeded the World Trade Organization from meeting in Seattle. The Battle of Seattle confirmed that anti-capitalist struggles were here to stay.

Ten differences between the traditional Left and new anti-capitalism

The new anti-capitalism has inherited traditions from previous struggles in history. And yet it is different: it has learned from the past and adapted to the present.

1. Taking power?

Despite differences between past Leftist traditions, they have one thing in common: they all pledged to transform society by *taking power*. Their strategy was to take over *political power* and use the State as a *tool* to emancipate society.

THERE IS SOME CONFUSION REGARDING THIS CONCEPT. EVEN IF WE WANTED TO "TAKE POWER," WHO SAID THAT POWER IS ONLY POLITICAL, AND CONCENTRATED IN THE STATE?

AND EVEN IF IT WAS, WHO SAID THAT STATE POWER IS IN THE HANDS OF THE NATION-STATES?

Nation-states only control a portion of what we call *political power*—the ability to impose norms to regulate social life. The governments of the most powerful nations, large businesses, financial corporations, and the mass media control more aspects of power than do most Nation-states. By taking over the *State*, we would only be taking control of a portion of *political power*.

However, power is much more than what we understand by *political power*. Power is not only present in the State or large corporations: it is in how we think, in our daily activities, in the way we relate to each other, in the way we perceive our peers, in our language, and in our identities. Power penetrates the totality of social relations, even those that the oppressed establish among themselves.

POWER ISN'T SOMETHING THAT INVADES US "FROM THE OUTSIDE"; ON THE CONTRARY, WE HAVE INTERNALIZED AND INCORPORATED POWER. POWER CONTROLS SOCIAL LIFE AND PEOPLE'S LIVES "FROM THE INSIDE." IT WOULD BE MORE APPROPRIATE TO CALL IT BIO-POWER, BECAUSE IT ABSORBS SOCIAL LIFE AND EVEN INDIVIDUAL LIFE, GIVING IT A NEW FORM. NOT ONLY DOES IT CONTROL LIFE, BUT ALSO ATTEMPTS TO RECREATE IT ACCORDING TO ITS IMAGE AND LIKENESS.

Michel Foucault

Power doesn't have a center: it is present everywhere and manifests itself in a thousand ways. Power isn't a thing or an institution, but a *continual process* of separating people and taking away their ability to run their own lives. Therein lies the difficulty of "taking power": taking control of the *State* doesn't mean taking power.

The new anti-capitalism rejects the idea of "taking power" not only because it's not possible, but also because sometimes it is *undesirable*. Power transforms everything around it: that is its most effective trick to neutralize its enemies. In an attempt to take over the State apparatus, social movements have often ended up recreating and even fortifying power relations. In order to win elections or "seize" the State, anti-capitalists in the past organized parties or liberation armies that were in themselves machines to divide, discipline and subordinate people. And the few times they were able to take over the State, they invariably created forms of oppression that were more intense and sophisticated than the previous ones.

THIS IS WHY, BEFORE "TAKING POWER," THE NEW ANTI-CAPITALISM TRIES TO AVOID BEING TAKEN OVER BY POWER. IT'S ABOUT CREATING SOCIAL RELATIONS WHERE POWER DISAPPEARS OR IS LIMITED. IT'S MORE ABOUT "DISEMPOWERING" THE STATE THAN IT IS ABOUT "TAKING OVER" IT.

SOME CALL THIS PERSPECTIVE "POPULAR POWER" WHILE OTHERS PREFER TO CALL IT "ANTI-POWER" OR "COUNTER-POWER" IT'S THE SAME TO ME.

2. Autonomy

If power is everywhere and penetrates everything, and no "taking" of power would solve that, how can we fight capitalism? What exactly is popular power, or counter-power?

For the new anti-capitalism, the answer to this question is in the very word *power*, which has two opposite meanings. As a noun, *power* refers to the social relationship of command and obedience, or having *power over* others. As a verb, *power* refers to the capacity to create and develop activities; it is what we are *capable of doing*.

IT IS WHAT I CALL "POSSE."

AND WHAT I CALL POWER-TO. POWER-OVER LIMITS OUR DOING, BUT ALSO LIVES OFF OF IT, AS IF IT WERE A VAMPIRE. IT CONTROLS US, BUT IT ALSO LIVES OFF OF OUR DOING.

John Holloway

Antonio Negri

The two meanings are opposed because one negates the other. *Power-over* limits freedom of doing everything that one could do (if one wasn't submitted to the power of others); the expansion of *power-to* undermines *power-over*, because it implies breaking the limits that are imposed over the *doing*.

90

Like power, resistance is everywhere and penetrates all social corners of life. Wherever there is power, there is resistance.

Men and women have struggled in thousands of ways against power in order to reclaim their ability to act. Sometimes they resist without knowing it: the worker who constantly changes jobs in search of better conditions; the exile who leaves his or her country for a less oppressive one; the deserting soldier who refuses to obey orders; a woman who leaves her exploitive husband; the artists who lives a non-commercial life, etc. In all of these cases, individuals tried to avoid being *taken* by power.

New anti-capitalism tries to encourage this resistance with the aim of developing our power to act freely. *Popular power,* or *counter-power,* refers to the struggle to extend *autonomy* to the oppressed and the possibility to live by rules which *we set*. On the contrary, power always entails *heteronomy*, subjection to rules we didn't decide on.

Each time an *autonomous* space is created, a place for *shared life*, it opens a crack in the capitalist system.

When workers organize themselves to defend their rights; when peasants take over land; when squatters convert an abandoned house into a cultural center; when indigenous people defend their rights to conserve their traditions; when the unemployed develop self-managed economic projects; in all of these cases, resistance *against* capitalism becomes a struggle *for* autonomy.

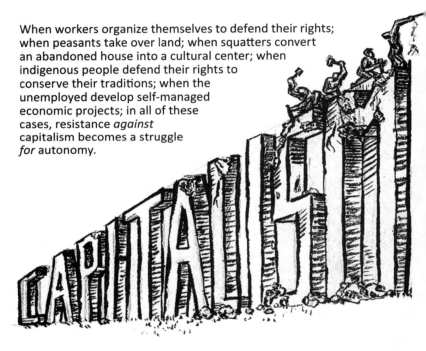

For the new anti-capitalism, it's about permanently trying to wedge open the cracks of autonomy that resistance opens in all parts of capitalist power.

Every time that men and women discover ways to escape oppression and live according to their own rules, capitalist power is forced to find new ways to dominate them, through advances in technology, transformations in production, and political power organization.

The politics of new anti-capitalism seek to increase and strengthen our ability for self-determination, that's to say, for *autonomy*. When we are called upon to *obey* decisions that *others* make—whether it's the State or a political party that claims to represent our interests—that's when autonomy is threatened.

Does this mean we cannot have any relationship to political power, or that we shouldn't try to use any space or resource connected with the State?

OF COURSE NOT. WE SHOULD PLAN OUT THE ANTI-CAPITALIST STRATEGY ACCORDING TO EACH SITUATION: SOMETIMES IT CAN BE USEFUL TO PARTICIPATE IN AN ELECTION OR OCCUPY A SPACE WITHIN THE STATE, MAYBE EVEN THE ENTIRE STATE. BUT ONLY WHEN IT IS CLEAR THAT IT IS NOT THE OVERALL POLITICAL TACTIC.

ANY DECISION THAT IS TAKEN SHOULD HAVE THE FUNCTION OF DEVELOPING AUTONOMY BEYOND THE STATE. ANY KIND OF POLITICS THAT MAKE "TAKING POWER" A PRIORITY AND THAT CHANGE THINGS FROM "THE TOP DOWN" THREATENS AUTONOMY, BECAUSE POWER AND THE STATE ARE MECHANISMS THAT IMPEDE AUTONOMOUS DEVELOPMENT. OCCUPYING GOVERNMENT POSITIONS CAN BE USEFUL IN ELIMINATING OBSTACLES IN THE ROAD TO EMANCIPATION, BUT AN EMANCIPATED WORLD CANNOT BE CONSTRUCTED FROM THE STATE.

✖ FOR MORE INFORMATION ON AUTONOMY
http://www.commoner.org.uk/
http://www.elkilombo.org/

3. Revolution is today

The perspective of *popular power* or *counter-power* supposes a profound change in the way in which we imagine revolution. A *revolution* means a radical and long-lasting change in social relations. This is what Marx, for example, meant when he used the word in "the Industrial Revolution." An *anti-capitalist* revolution implies that this change disarticulates or destroys capitalist relations.

Mesmerized by the myth of the French Revolution and by the idea of "taking power," the old Left conceived a mistaken image of what revolutions look like.

IN PLACE OF A RADICAL CHANGE IN SOCIAL RELATIONS, THE LEFT CONCEIVED OF REVOLUTIONS AS A PARTICULAR POLITICAL EVENT. THE REVOLUTION WOULD OCCUR WHEN A PARTY OR SOCIAL MOVEMENT TAKES CONTROL OF THE STATE APPARATUS.

The new anti-capitalism knows that taking the State does not imply a radical change in social relations. Often, these supposed "revolutions" were nothing more than a transfer of elites, without any profound societal changes taking place. True revolutions do not have a precise date or hour, even though particular political events can fundamentally affect their development. For example, the *bourgeois revolutions,* which put an end to feudalism, were long processes of social change. In many cases, they required *several* "seizures of power," and in other cases they did not need *any.*

For the new anti-capitalism the revolution isn't a *future* event that we must *wait* for. The revolution is in an ongoing process, which occurs every day, each time men and women develop new ways of resisting power and create new spaces of autonomy. Each time they create self-managed, noncommercial, and egalitarian spaces, the revolution is taking place. The revolution results from what the *community* of struggling produces, and establishment of new social relations.

Antonio Negri

THIS IS WHAT I CALL DEVELOPING "COMMUNISM HERE AND NOW." THIS HAS NOTHING TO DO WITH WHAT IS COMMONLY CALLED "REFORMISM." REFORMISM CONSISTS OF INTRODUCING GRADUAL REFORMS FROM THE STATE, TO GLOSS OVER THE MOST HARMFUL ASPECTS OF CAPITALISM, WITHOUT CHANGING SOCIAL RELATIONS. "COMMUNISM HERE AND NOW" MEANS THE OPPOSITE: IT MEANS BUILDING AUTONOMY AND CONFRONTING POWER ON A DAILY BASIS.

SO THEN, YOU MEAN TO SAY THAT THERE WILL BE NO MORE EVENTS LIKE POLITICAL REVOLUTIONS? ANTI-CAPITALISTS SHOULDN'T FOSTER THEM?

NO WAY. IT IS LIKELY THAT ON MANY OCCASIONS WE WILL HAVE TO REBEL AGAINST A GOVERNMENT OR EVEN "SEIZE THE STATE."

HOWEVER IT'S BEST TO UNDERSTAND THAT A REVOLUTION ISN'T A PARTICULAR EVENT, BUT A PROFOUND AND WIDESPREAD PROCESS OF SOCIAL CHANGE.

Highlighting the continuous *day to day* character of the revolution doesn't mean that profound *breaks* aren't necessary. Many times, in our daily resistance, social movements invent new ways to resist, or generate unexpected or unplanned events. These breaks are needed to move from resistance to the construction of a new world.

4. Horizontalism

The idea of "the revolution today" implies that the *practices* and forms of organization of the new anti-capitalist struggles *anticipate* or *prefigure* the kind of society that we wish to create. By considering struggles and organizations as mere *means* that would allow us to meet a *future end* (the revolution), the traditional Left has neglected the library potential that our own organization and struggle can offer. Under the guise of "efficiency," they created hierarchical, oppressive, competitive, and discriminatory strategies and forms of organizing.

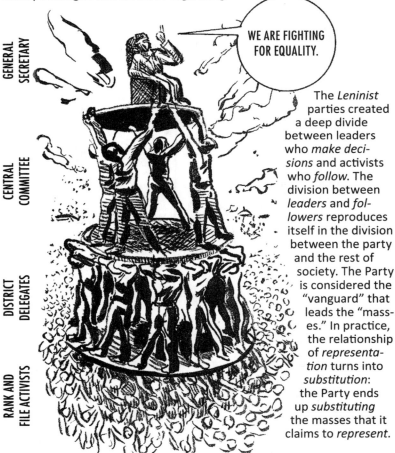

GENERAL SECRETARY

CENTRAL COMMITTEE

DISTRICT DELEGATES

RANK AND FILE ACTIVISTS

WE ARE FIGHTING FOR EQUALITY.

The *Leninist* parties created a deep divide between leaders who *make decisions* and activists who *follow*. The division between *leaders* and *followers* reproduces itself in the division between the party and the rest of society. The Party is considered the "vanguard" that leads the "masses." In practice, the relationship of *representation* turns into *substitution*: the Party ends up *substituting* the masses that it claims to *represent*.

This kind of hierarchical organization, in which it demands the *exclusive* membership of activists (no one can belong to more than one party), often produces competitive relations based on mistrust and sectarianism, rather than cooperation, solidarity, and unity despite differences.

Each party tries to accumulate supporters, fearing that another party will steal them away. Each member must constantly show *loyalty* and may fear that his or her opinions will create suspicion among his or her comrades.

The new anti-capitalism knows that if the idea is to create a more equal, autonomous, free world based on mutual solidarity, one can't start by fostering the opposite values. The *means should coincide with the end.* The *community* of those who struggle—including their strategies and organizational structures—should *anticipate* the kind of world they want to build.

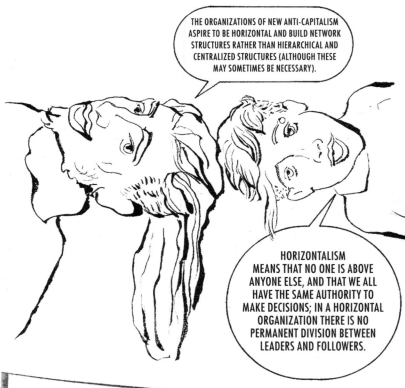

THE ORGANIZATIONS OF NEW ANTI-CAPITALISM ASPIRE TO BE HORIZONTAL AND BUILD NETWORK STRUCTURES RATHER THAN HIERARCHICAL AND CENTRALIZED STRUCTURES (ALTHOUGH THESE MAY SOMETIMES BE NECESSARY).

HORIZONTALISM MEANS THAT NO ONE IS ABOVE ANYONE ELSE, AND THAT WE ALL HAVE THE SAME AUTHORITY TO MAKE DECISIONS; IN A HORIZONTAL ORGANIZATION THERE IS NO PERMANENT DIVISION BETWEEN LEADERS AND FOLLOWERS.

There is a debate within the new anti-capitalism. Some think that horizontalism means a rejection of all forms of *representation,* while others think that it is useful to elect representatives with limited powers. To prevent being *replaced by representatives,* participants may elect *representatives* for limited nonrenewable terms, any representative can be revoked, and the roles that the representatives fill can be rotated or picked at random, etc.

However, horizontalism isn't limited to a democratic, *assembly*-based organizational principle. It also implies making permanent efforts to eliminate any kind of *elitism* or *hierarchy* among members. In any group there are people who have more education, experience, economic recourses, better contacts, more energy, or simply more charisma than others. These differences may imply that those who have more skills or resources can influence decisions more than everyone else. Horizontalism consists of a completely different *culture*, one that aspires for everyone to have the same opportunities to make their point of view heard, so that no one can *accumulate* more authority than others. That's why horizontal organization puts so much emphasis on the *socialization* of *knowledge* and *resources*.

5. Network structures

Autonomy and horizontalism has two enemies: big numbers and far distances. It is very difficult to maintain an effective horizontal organization if hundreds of people participate, or if they don't live close enough to meet regularly. When this is the case, someone often proposes to create a *hierarchical structure* or to *centralize* the leadership of a group to gain efficiency. To solve this dilemma, the new anti-capitalism has developed coordination and network structures. A network is a series of *voluntary* relationships and *connections* between people or *autonomous* organizations.

A NETWORK DOESN'T HAVE A CENTRAL HEAD OR DECISION MAKER, NOR DOES IT HAVE A CENTRAL COMMAND OR HIERARCHIES. WE ARE THE NETWORK, ALL OF US WHO SPEAK AND LISTEN.

Subcomandante Marcos

A network is established when participating groups or *node groups* find that they have a common interest and they can exchange information or resources or act coordinately. Nodes may debate from afar and arrive at a consensus that allows them to make unified decisions. But this doesn't imply that each actor loses or *delegates* its capacity to decide for himself or herself: horizontalism and autonomy preserve it.

In contrast to networks, hierarchal and centralized organizations typical of the traditional Left have a tree-like structure: an exclusive "central tree trunk" out of which "main branches" grow, and from those "smaller branches." Compared to the "tree/branch" structures, networks have a series of advantages; for example, they allow for *free* and *continuous communication*, because each node can establish *horizontal* relationships with one another freely. On the contrary, the branches of a tree can only communicate "vertically," having *first* gone through the trunk. For example, if the centralized decision-making body and communication body of a party decides to *block* a proposal from a regional committee, or simply veto it, the flow of communication is interrupted.

NETWORKS ALSO FACILITATE CREATIVITY AND INNOVATION. EVERY NODE CAN EXPLORE AND REINVENT NEW PATHS. IT'S PROBABLE, AMONG THOUSANDS OF NODES, SOME WILL TUMBLE ONTO A GREAT DISCOVERY, MAYBE EVEN BY ACCIDENT. IF A DISCOVERY IS USEFUL, MANY OTHER POINTS IN THE NETWORK CAN TAKE ADVANTAGE OF IT, ADAPT IT AND TRANSFORM IT INTO A GLOBAL INNOVATION.

NO ONE CAN PREDICT HOW A NETWORK WILL ACT IN ANY PARTICULAR MOMENT. THAT'S ITS GREAT STRENGTH!

John Jordan (1965-)

Central structures discourage local creativity and innovation, because everyone is waiting for things to come from "the top."

Networks are more sensitive to *realities* and *local needs* and facilitate the creation of *alliances* that are *more flexible* and *pluralistic*. For example, the *central committee* of a party can decide not to establish contacts with a particular political group. But maybe in some region, for particular reasons, these relationships would be indispensable. In this case, a node wouldn't think twice about joining a network, while the "branch" of the tree must wait for the "trunk" to listen to the proposal and approve the relationship.

Also, on the contrary of what is generally believed, centralized and hierarchical structures are much more *vulnerable* than networks.

SINCE EACH NODE OF A NETWORK CAN OPERATE AUTONOMOUSLY, THE NETWORK CAN STILL ENDURE EVEN IF ONE OR SEVERAL PARTS ARE DESTROYED.

GIVEN THAT NO SINGLE NODE IS INDISPENSIBLE FOR THE OTHERS TO CONTINUE TO BUILD RELATIONSHIPS, IT'S VERY DIFFICULT TO FULLY DESTROY A NETWORK. THIS IS WHAT WE CALL A "RHIZOMATIC STRUCTURE."

Gilles Deleuze
(1925-1995)

Félix Guattari
(1930-1992)

On the contrary, a treelike structure would collapse if the center breaks or is attacked. The annals of union organizations and the Left are filled with stories of "bureaucratization," "tragic errors," or "betrayal" from leaders that jeopardized entire movements. For the new anti-capitalism, it's simply not necessary that the fate of the struggle should be controlled by a *center*, or left to a handful of people who could easily make mistakes, become corrupt, or be destroyed.

Another advantage of building network structures is the way in which they grow. Political parties, for example, grow through *accumulation*. They put emphasis on accumulating supporters and more members, or acquiring more resources. Networks behave like living organisms, which expand, creating new autonomous organizations. Like cells, networks grow by *multiplying* and by creating *new nodes*; not from accumulating more people or resources of *one* group. The more nodes, and more diverse they are, the stronger the network.

THIS FOSTERS COOPERATION AND SOLIDARITY. AND NO NODE HAS A REASON TO FEAR THE CREATION OF NEW NODES, UNLIKE THE PARTIES, WHICH PERCEIVE THE GROWTH OF ANOTHER PARTY AS A THREAT.

THIS IS WHY MOST NEW ANTI-CAPITALIST ORGANIZATIONS DO NOT TO REQUIRE THAT PARTICIPANTS BECOME EXCLUSIVE MEMBERS; EACH MEMBER CAN PARTICIPATE IN MORE THAN ONE COLLECTIVE. .

The preference of network structures doesn't mean fully rejecting centralization of structures. Sometimes some level of centralization is necessary and useful in particular circumstances. What is important is not to subject networks to a permanent center or authority.

6. Multiplicity

One fundamental difference between the new anti-capitalism and previous Leftist traditions is the debate over the subject, or, in other words, the question of what social group will lead us toward emancipation. It is a big issue, because it guides all political actions.

The national liberation movements, for example, placed all of their hope on "the People," conceived as a block of peasants, workers, small businessmen, and everyone who defended "national interests" against imperialism.

The traditional Left preferred to trust the industrial "working class" as the historical agent capable of leading the struggle against the bourgeoisie.

The new anti-capitalism conceives the subject as something more unde-fined, mobile, plural and ubiquitous than the traditional Left. Capitalism affects most human beings, although in very different ways.

Workers—not just industrial workers—have good reasons to fight against the system that exploits them. But so do *peasants* and *indigenous peo-ples*, *ethnic and national minorities* that are discriminated against and at-tacked, *women, consumers, artists, journalists,* and *intellectuals, students* and *users of public services, environmentalists, human rights activists* and *pacifists,* and many other people. Capitalism is not only violent, dividing and exploiting us, but it also takes away our ability to make decisions over crucial aspects of our lives.

The traditional Left established a *hierarchy* between the different subjects' interests: the most important was the working class, or the interests of the "People." The rest would have *to wait* for their demands to be met until the "Revolution" comes along and brings happiness to everyone. Meanwhile, they would have to be *subordinated* to the working class or "national" struggles.

The new anti-capitalism rejects the idea that there is a *privileged* subject, who is predestined to emancipate everyone else: emancipation is thought of as the result of the struggles of each subject who fights in his or her own way. For the traditional Left, this *multiplicity* is an obstacle to the homogenization and discipline that the strategy of "taking power" requires. On the contrary, the new anti-capitalism *stimulates* the multiplicity, because it strengthens our struggles.

THAT IS WHY I SAY THAT IT'S ABOUT CREATING ONE WORLD IN WHICH MANY WORLDS FIT.

Subcomandante Marcos

For the new anti-capitalism, the *unity in diversity* is achieved by negotiating *differences*. The *articulation* of the different subjects is only achieved through *mutual recognition*. When they meet in the struggle, on equal ground, each subject has the possibility of *recognizing* the validity of each others' demands, projects, and forms of organizing.

Subjects "adapt" to one another to be able to march together. Recognizing the other isn't just acceptance, but also "allowing one to be contaminated" by it.

For the new anti-capitalism, changing the world is too important to leave it only in the hands of activists. Moreover, it's about creating spaces for the anti-capitalist that most people have inside them—even the people who say they aren't interested in "politics"—can come out. Building an anti-capitalism that is able to speak the language of the common people involves:

✖ *Worrying about the people and their concrete problems, rather than considering them simple objects to use for political objectives*;

✖ *Creating forms of struggle that will allow* everyone to get involved according to their possibilities and desires, without the need to give up the obligations and pleasures of their private lives;

✖ *Working consistently and patiently* in popular education.

The recognition of the *multiple* and *plural* nature of the political subject also implies changes in the way decisions are made. Many groups and networks from the new anti-capitalism movement prefer making decisions by consensus, rather than by majority "rule" or minority "loss." The effort to meet a consensus *also* satisfies the needs of the minority, which is part of the effort in considering the *other,* rather than discarding its opinions.

BUT MAKING DECISIONS BY CONSENSUS TAKES A LOT OF TIME!

THAT'S RIGHT. BUT IF WE WANT TO ADVANCE TOGETHER, WE HAVE TO WALK AT THE PACE OF THE SLOWEST ONE.

Subcomandante Marcos

This plural and multiple subject still doesn't have a name, maybe it doesn't need one. Some have called it "the multitude," to reflect that it is not one or several stable classes, but rather that it has a multiple character. "Multitude" is preferred over "people," because the latter refers to a group of people formed and recognized as such by a nation-state. A multitude struggles beyond—and many times even against and from outside—the borders of nation-states.

7. Political action tailored for every situation

New anti-capitalism prefers to define its strategies and political actions according to each situation. This means that it is better to organize struggles while paying close attention to the local situation, characteristics of the very group struggling, and the type of struggle they are carrying out.

IT IS NOT THE SAME TO FIGHT CAPITALISM IN A COUNTRY WHERE PEOPLE HAVE A LOT OF LEGAL RIGHTS THAN IN A COUNTRY WHERE THERE IS STRONG REPRESSION.

Naomi Klein
(1970-)

A STRATEGY CARRIED OUT BY A MOVEMENT OF UNEMPLOYED IS NOT THE SAME AS ONE CARRIED OUT BY PEASANTS, WORKERS, OR CONSUMERS.

GLOBAL RESISTANCE SHOULD BE BASED ON EACH LOCAL SITUATION. IT WOULDN'T MAKE SENSE FOR OUR STRUGGLES TO STAY SAME IN EVERY PLACE, LIKE A MCDONALD'S HAMBURGER.

On the contrary, the old Left tends to always use the same tactics: they need each situation to fit into the party's "program," and thus often disregard the specifics of the situation. The old Left always knows "what to do," without needing to reflect on the action or decision.

Secondly, having "a political action for each situation" means fighting against concrete manifestations of capitalism and the way they affect the lives of a particular group of people. For each place and time, it's about boosting the possibility for liberation, self-organization, and learning that each situation offers. The achievement of single objectives (even the ones that seem small), the development of new and improved ways of life, and building organization can be of value themselves. On the contrary, the old Left often fights against a *general* and *abstract* idea of "the capitalist system," dismissing the specific accomplishments of each concrete struggle.

The traditional Left is only interested in struggles if they adapt to their "program," adopt their slogans, and consist of an "advance" along the road toward their final goal, abolishing the "capitalist system." And as they believe they "know" more than everyone else about what to do and how to do it, they sometimes try to manipulate concrete struggles so that they fit within their "program" and their own *power strategy*.

In the politics of the traditional Left, people and organizations involved in each struggle end up being considered as simply *objects* for *general political* ends The traditional Leftist militant hopes to obtain *more* than what is at play in the particular situation of a struggle. And struggles are only "useful" if they are pushed in the direction hoped for. If the struggle doesn't meet the desired objective, the subjects are blamed for "not being prepared," or lack of "consciousness" and "direction."

THE BIGGEST PROBLEM IN HOW WE APPROACH POLITICS IS THAT MANY TIMES THE RESISTANCE OR STRUGGLES OF THE MULTITUDE END UP BEING SUBORDINATED TO A PROGRAM, PARTY, STATE, OR LEADER THAT SQUASHES THE POSSIBILITIES FOR THE DEVELOPMENT OF AUTONOMOUS AND CREATIVE POTENTIAL THAT THE STRUGGLES HAVE.

BY BEING FORCED INTO A PREESTABLISHED MODEL OF ORGANIZATION, CONSCIOUSNESS, AND STRUGGLE, THE CREATIVE CAPABILITIES OF THE SUBJECTS TURN OUT TO BE LIMITED OR DEPLETED.

So, are general ideas worthless? Can people in one situation learn from people in another? Of course they can. But there are fundamental differences in the attitudes of the activists. A traditional militant tends to participate in situations of struggle "from the outside," and tells everyone else what they should do, how to do it, and shows them the "right" approach to things; he or she always has an opinion about everything.

On the contrary, the new anti-capitalist activist knows that listening is more important than speaking well. He or she uses past experiences accrued from past struggles or from life experience, acting more as a cultural "mediator" who connects knowledge acquired from different situations of struggle and makes it available for everyone else. One "learns" from each situation what the most appropriate political action is.

These two activist models are related to different conceptions of what "the truth" is and how to define "what is correct" in politics. The traditional Left tends to consider that there exists a single "objective truth," that is beyond all the different points of view. This "truth" is what indicates the correct strategy; those who know the truth are those who "know" what political actions to take.

In general, the new anti-capitalist activists prefer to separate the issue. A *correct* political decision is one that, more than anything, is agreed upon through consensus by those struggling within a particular situation. Even if there was *one* truth—and many doubt that this is the case—it could only arise from each situation. And no one can have the pretension of "knowing more" or that he or she "knows better" than everyone else.

ALSO, AN ELEMENT OF "NOT KNOWING" IS FUNDAMENTAL IN BEING ABLE TO ADAPT OR TO EVOLVE.

WHOEVER THINKS THAT HE OR SHE KNOWS EVERYTHING DOESN'T WORRY ABOUT LISTENING OR TRYING TO UNDERSTAND MORE.

ASKING, WE WALK.

Subcomandante Marcos

8. Globalizing the struggle

Since its origins, the traditional Left understood that capitalism is a *global* system, and that the struggle against it could triumph only if it was *internationalist*. However, the Left's commitment to internationalism began to decay over time.

✘ During World War I, the Social Democrats gave into patriotism and supported the war.

✘ The national liberation movements adopted a strong nationalist discourse to fight against *imperialism*.

✘ The Leninist tendency of the Left maintained an internationalist perspective, but as they believed that they would have to seize the State (national), they almost always preferred to support actions *within a national territory*.

THE NEW ANTI-CAPITALISM HAS REVISITED AND EXPLORED THE INTERNATIONALISM THAT THE LEFT HAS ALWAYS CULTIVATED IN THEIR THEORIES, AS WELL AS IN THEIR STRATEGIES AND WAYS OF ORGANIZING.

THE USE OF THE INTERNET AND NETWORK STRUCTURES IS ALLOWING MAGNIFICENT EXPERIENCES OF COORDINATION OF DIVERSE GROUPS ON A GLOBAL SCALE, VISIBLE IN THE RISE OF A NEW GLOBAL RESISTANCE MOVEMENT.

Many authors have pointed out the uselessness of placing our hope on change within a *national* arena, because *globalization* has irreversibly reduced the decision-making power of nation-states.

THE ERA OF IMPERIALISM HAS ENDED. TODAY, CAPITALISM HAS CONSOLIDATED INTO AN EMPIRE, A STRUCTURE OF GLOBAL POWER THAT DOES NOT HAVE A CENTER NOR IS DETERMINED BY TERRITORIAL LIMITS. THE EMPIRE IS ORGANIZED IN A NETWORK OF NATIONAL AND TRANSNATIONAL INSTITUTIONS—THE UNITED NATIONS, NATO, THE IMF, A HANDFUL OF POWERFUL STATES, MULTINATIONAL CORPORATIONS, AND SEVERAL NON-GOVERNMENTAL ORGANIZATIONS, ETC. CAPITAL CIRCULATES FREELY IN THE WORLD, AND MEANWHILE, THE EMPIRE TRIES TO GUARANTEE CONDITIONS FOR REPRODUCTION.

Michael Hardt (1960-)

Antonio Negri

This is why anti-capitalists today tend to put less effort into organizing struggles in a *national* confine. They focus on two other spaces: the *local*—region, city, neighborhood, workplace, etc.—and *global*—struggles against international corporations coordinated globally, actions against summit meetings, transnational unionization, etc.

117

As *capitalism* doesn't have a center, and as the nation-states serve as *machines to divide* people (in addition to losing a large part of their attributions), *globalizing the struggles* is an imperious necessity. The globalization of anti-capitalist resistance (or "globalization from below") means attacking capitalism everywhere. Also anti-capitalism must not accept the political conditions imposed, for example, when the State establishes that a person loses all political rights if he or she leaves the territory occupied by a nation-state.

GLOBALIZING THE STRUGGLE MEANS ESTABLISHING SOLIDARITY AND BUILDING STRONG COMMUNITY RELATIONSHIPS BETWEEN ALL THE OPPRESSED, NO MATTER WHERE THEY WERE BORN. IT MEANS RECOGNIZING THAT IF WE ARE DIVIDED AND SEPARATED WE WILL NEVER DEFEAT CAPITALISM.

LET THE RESISTANCE BE AS GLOBAL AS CAPITAL!

Globalizing the resistance doesn't necessarily imply forgetting about political actions within a nation, much less dissolving or opposing elements of everyone's unique *national culture*. It means articulating our *local struggles* with *the* perspectives and networks of global resistance, without losing local "flavor" and "color."

9. Direct Action and civil disobedience

The new anti-capitalism respects the principle of *plurality of tactics*: each group can fight in the ways they want to and need to. We do not need to do everything in the same way in order for us to do things *together*. However, there are some tactics emphasized within new anti-capitalism: *direct actions* and civil disobedience. *Direct actions* means that one carries out actions necessary to force a change *oneself*, rather than waiting for authorities to act. When we vote for a candidate who promises to do something that we want, when we collect signatures or send petitions to government, we are utilizing *indirect* tactics: we are *asking* for *others* to do something for *us*.

> I'VE LISTENED TO YOUR DEMANDS, NOW GO BACK HOME AND I'LL TAKE CARE OF THINGS.

> I'LL HANDLE THINGS THE WAY THAT I WANT TO, HA!

> IF THIS POLITICIAN DOESN'T KEEPS HIS PROMISE, NEXT TIME I'LL PROPOSE DIRECT ACTION: FOR EXAMPLE, BLOCKING THE ENTRANCE TO THE GOVERNMENT BUILDING.

Direct action means departing from political *passivity* and doing things *oneself*, or carrying out an action that *forces* authorities to work in a desired way.

Civil disobedience involves actions in which people break laws openly and collectively. Many *direct actions* are forms of *civil disobedience* and vice versa. One example includes the Italian *Disobedientes* tactic of invading concentration camps where illegal immigrants are held to liberate them. However, not all direct actions necessarily break the law, nor are they always political or open actions. Not all forms of disobedience are supposed to be actions: sometimes it's about *passively* resisting a law.

I OPENLY AND PUBLICALLY REFUSE TO KILL FELLOW HUMAN BEINGS IN THE NAME OF THE STATE.

I DON'T CARE: YOU'LL HAVE TO PUT MY ENTIRE BATTALION IN JAIL BECAUSE WE'VE ALL DECIDED TO DISOBEY.

WELL THEN, YOU'RE GOING TO PRISON FOR BETRAYING YOUR COUNTRY.

It is important to distinguish these types of tactics from the tactics predominantly used among the traditional Left, which are often based on "indirect" actions and electoral campaigns. When carried out well, *direct actions* and *civil disobedience* can bring concrete and immediate results. They allow us to challenge the limits of what is allowed, and they give people participating in the struggles something real, a sense of agency.

BUT ISN'T IT ANTI-DEMOCRATIC THAT WHAT YOU WANT IS AGAINST THE LAW?

OF COURSE NOT: IF DEMOCRACY TRULY EXISTED, OUR TACTICS WOULDN'T BE JUSTIFIED. BUT THAT ISN'T THE CASE.

SO, YOU THINK THAT YOU HAVE THE RIGHT TO DO WHATEVER YOU WANT, WITHOUT ANY LIMITS?

OF COURSE NOT: ALL OUR ACTIONS ARE FOUNDED ON ETHICAL GROUNDS. THE ENDS DO NOT JUSTIFY THE MEANS: LEGITIMATE ENDS NEED MEANS THAT ARE PERCEIVED AS LEGITIMATE.

The new anti-capitalism considers that we live under a *dictatorship of capital*. That's why *direct actions* and *civil disobedience* can be illegal, but still *legitimate*. This doesn't mean that anti-capitalists can do whatever they feel like: part of the fundamental political actions of the new anti-capitalism is *building the legitimacy* of their actions. It's about establishing a continuous flow of communication with society, a "back and forth," a way for large portions of the population to approve (or at least not reject) the demands as well as the methods used to make them heard.

✖ PRACTICAL ADVICE ABOUT DIRECT ACTION AND CIVIL DISOBEDIENCE
www.starhawk.org/activism/activism.html
www.actupny.org/documents/CDdocuments/Guidelines.html
www.ruckus.org/section.php?id=82

10. Creativity and happiness

One of the most important differences between the new anti-capitalism and the traditional Left is something difficult to define because it's not found in books or theories, but in *activist culture*.

In conceiving emancipatory politics not as a *war*, but as an effort to permanently *create*, the relationships between activists and political activity change sensibly.

✖ THE TRADITIONAL LEFT Culture of War	✖ NEW ANTI-CAPITALISM Culture of Creation
Values "sacrifice" for a cause.	Values creation and living happy and full lives.
Individual interests are dissolved into the collective interests.	The collective includes and accepts individual interests.
Disapproval of doubts and hesitation.	Accepts "not knowing" as a fundamental part of life.
Private life is secondary.	Private life is fundamental.
Intolerance of weakness and error.	Understanding that mistakes are a part of life.
Values fearlessness without measuring consequences.	Values courage accompanied by prudence.
Culture of turning the dead or victims into "heroes" and "martyrs."	Reveres the lives of those who struggle every day.
Activists are separated from common people.	Integrated participants.
Rigid discipline.	Flexible commitment.

As the revolution is *today*, for the new anti-capitalism happiness is not something that is discovered or will occur when we get to the end of the road. The *community* of activists in *itself* has a happy, satisfying, and personally gratifying ambience.

This activist culture is reflected in many of the struggles and actions carried out by the new anti-capitalism, for example festivals, and artistic tactics used during actions to make police repression more difficult (such as dressing up as clowns, giving out flowers, street theater performances, etc.).

This new activist culture is also reflected in the close relationship between *art* and *politics*. The "warlike" activist culture of the traditional Left reduced using art in the best of cases as an "accessory." But as the main task of activists is to create a new world *here* and *now*, the new anti-capitalism shares the work of artists. *Creativity* is something they both share.

WORKSHOP FOR CREATING A NEW WORLD

Political art groups have played a fundamental role in many of the new anti-capitalist struggles. The anti-capitalist movement increasingly uses art in popular education, to send messages, and during direct actions.

Anti-capitalism's new movements, networks, and actions

Not all concrete examples offered in the following pages have the characteristics of the new anti-capitalism (some of the struggles don't even call themselves "anti-capitalist"). Some are small movements, while others are massive. Some have lasted decades, while others have had a short life.

However, the purity of these examples is not what is important, nor the words they use to identify themselves; much less is it their size or lifespan.

The selected cases exemplify the potential for the growth of a massive and widespread anti-capitalist movement. In their practical experience, these cases have created new subjectivities, opened new horizons, and developed new ways of struggling.

This is the value of the new anti-capitalism.

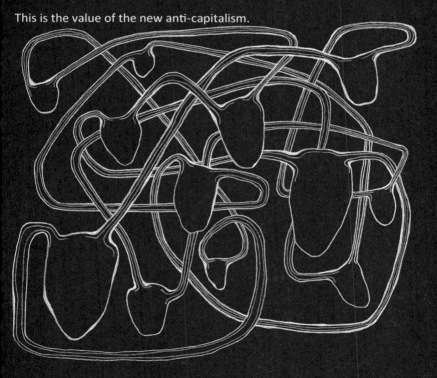

Indigenous people enter the stage: the Zapatistas

Even though different political groups contributed to the birth of new anti-capitalism, it was indigenous people who created the first visibly international movement. Denied rights for more than 500 years, subjected to white domination, and increasingly displaced by capitalist expansion, the indigenous people of Southern Mexico decided to actualize their long tradition of struggle to defend their way of life; but this time they did it in a new way.

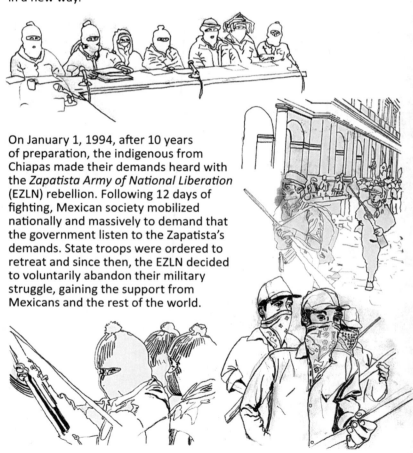

On January 1, 1994, after 10 years of preparation, the indigenous from Chiapas made their demands heard with the *Zapatista Army of National Liberation* (EZLN) rebellion. Following 12 days of fighting, Mexican society mobilized nationally and massively to demand that the government listen to the Zapatista's demands. State troops were ordered to retreat and since then, the EZLN decided to voluntarily abandon their military struggle, gaining the support from Mexicans and the rest of the world.

The Zapatista's political actions sum up many of the characteristics of new anti-capitalism. Even though they are an army and have adopted armed struggle as part of their tactics, their political ideology is far from militaristic.

THE FUTURE OF EZLN ISN'T DEFINED IN MILITARY TERMS, BUT IN POLITICAL TERMS. THE ENEMY DOES NOT WORRY US. WE ARE WORRIED ABOUT HOW WE DEFINE NEW RELATIONS BETWEEN COMPAÑEROS.

The Zapatistas firmly reject *hierarchies* and the idea of the *vanguard*. They prefer to make efforts to achieve *wide* consensus among social movements. For them, the idea is about "command by obeying," and "walking at the pace of the slowest one." The famous messages from their spokesperson, Subcomandante Marcos, with his pleasant tone and poetic prose, do not speak of destruction, but the construction of a new world based on *respect* for *diversity*. The Zapatistas reject the idea of imposing a "system" or a new "truth": for them it's about "creating one world in which many worlds fit."

The Zapatistas have declared that they do not propose to "take power"; rather, their goal is much more profound: *abolishing power relations*. For this, the Zapatista project also supports the idea of autonomy: the insurgent indigenous have worked to transform Chiapas into a liberated territory, one in which they can contribute daily to building the world in which they want to live. The revolution is neither an *event* nor an objective which to reach, but a continual *process* of creating a new world.

The recognition of the *diversity* of struggles, none of which can be considered a *priority*, continuously appears in the Zapatista discourse.

The Zapatistas were the first to contribute to building international networks that connected struggles from diverse places in the world. Supporting the call for an international network of movements, in July 1996 activists from more than 40 countries came to Chiapas to meet during the First Intercontinental Gathering for Humanity and Against Neo-liberalism. This meeting is considered the first international call against capitalist globalization.

CAPITALISM IS THE CAUSE OF MOST OF THE SUFFERING IN THE WORLD. BEYOND OUR DIFFERENCES, WE ARE UNITED BY ONE NO, AND MANY YESES.

In 1997, the Second Gathering took place, this time in Barcelona. From this meeting came the initiative to create Peoples' Global Action (PGA), one of the most important social movement networks in the world, which celebrated its first conference in 1998. Since then, the PGA has remained active and has been a guiding light for social activists from indigenous movements, peasant organizations, workers, and many others.

✖ CONTACTS
EZLN: *www.enlacezapatista.ezln.org.mx/*

✖ FOR MORE INFORMATION ABOUT INDIGENOUS MOVEMENTS
www.conaie.nativeweb.org
www.iwgia.org

Peasants defend their way of life: Landless Workers Movement and Via Campesina

Peasants have been some of the most active social subjects in the rise of the new anti-capitalist movement. The Landless Worker's Movement (MST) of Brazil, in which more than 1.5 million farmers from over 23 states participate, is a good example.

MST was formed in 1984, as a response to the advance of large land estates and mechanization in agriculture and land concentration implemented during the military dictatorship, which had displaced thousands of families from their lands.

MST developed its struggle for agrarian reform within a more general project for the creation of an egalitarian society "without exploiters," based on solidarity and "new values." The recuperation of "dignity" for the poor and oppressed is what MST means by a true "cultural revolution." Even though the organizational structure recognizes leaders, the role they have tends to be softer than other traditional movements; part of the important political work they are carrying out consists of developing the capacity for each peasant to make decisions using non-hierarchical methods and models.

Direct action is a fundamental part of MST's historic struggle. Throughout the organization's history, aside from carrying out marches and hunger strikes, they have occupied thousands of acres of private land, they have squatted haciendas, taken over public buildings and multinational offices, and they have even taken part in the destruction of genetically modified crop plantations.

Even though the MST participated in the formation of Brazil's *Worker's Party* (PT), it has maintained an autonomous space, without subordinating to the requirements and pace of electoral politics. The construction of *autonomous* spaces is an important part of MST's struggle. Part of its role is the organization of agro-producers and self-managed cooperatives which produce, commercialize, provide services and credit to small farmers, which free them from being subjugated to predatory companies. MST puts a lot of effort into education, building their own schools, another example of the development of autonomous projects. Internationalism, the defense of the environment, and gender equality are some of the central aspects of MST's politics.

Peasant organizations from all over the world, including the MST, have organized since 1992 and developed a worldwide movement called *Via Campesina* (VC). VC defines itself as an "autonomous" and "pluralistic" movement to coordinate the struggles of small and midsize agricultural producers against neoliberalism. Part of their demands include the defense of "food sovereignty" for all people, agrarian reform, "social ownership of land" and a decentralized sustainable peasant agriculture, gender equality, human rights, and the protection of "biodiversity."

VC has valued movement-building with other sectors of society from around the world, coordinating an international common struggle. That is why VC has had such an active role in the global resistance movement and has participated in summit actions like the *Seattle battle*, among others.

CONTACTS
MST: *www.mstbrazil.org*
Via Campesina: *www.viacampesina.org/en/*

* Protest slogan used by Via Campesina during the 1999 Seattle protests

Workers refuse to live in exclusion: the Piqueteros and Occupied Factory Movement

Workers are also one of the main social groups participating in the new anti-capitalism. Chronic unemployment, extreme poverty, and exclusion have driven some of the most radicalized experiences within the new anti-capitalist movement.

A good example is the *piqueteros* or *Unemployed Workers Movements* (MTD) of Argentina, which began organizing in 1997 in the deindustrialized suburbs of Greater Buenos Aires. MTD began organizing workers who had lost their jobs and youth who had never held a job.

WE AREN'T INTERESTED IN ACCUMULATING POWER, OR BEING A VANGUARD. WHAT IS IMPORTANT IS TO MULTIPLY THE ORGANIZATIONAL EXPERIENCES, MORE THAN THE NAME OF AN ORGANIZATION.

The main objectives were work, recuperating "dignity," and achieving "social change." MTD's organizational structure is *horizontal*: they function as an *assembly*, prefer to make *decisions by consensus,* and put a lot of energy into *popular education* projects, which creates a space in which everyone can participate in decision making. They reject "programs" and closed truths, and they prefer *multiplicity* and *diversity*.

The construction of *autonomy* is an orienting principle for their political actions. For MTD, it's about building new spaces and social ties that intertwine the struggle and help foster new non-capitalist relationships. This is why they say they do not participate in elections to win government positions. Fundamental to building "counter power" are *self-managed* economic projects such as bakeries, construction block production sites, etc, which MTD organized with egalitarian and noncommercial criteria.

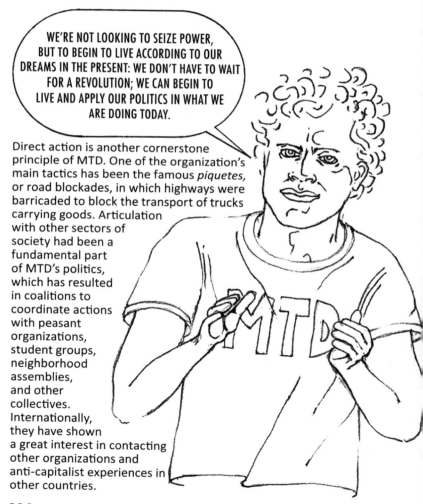

WE'RE NOT LOOKING TO SEIZE POWER, BUT TO BEGIN TO LIVE ACCORDING TO OUR DREAMS IN THE PRESENT: WE DON'T HAVE TO WAIT FOR A REVOLUTION; WE CAN BEGIN TO LIVE AND APPLY OUR POLITICS IN WHAT WE ARE DOING TODAY.

Direct action is another cornerstone principle of MTD. One of the organization's main tactics has been the famous *piquetes,* or road blockades, in which highways were barricaded to block the transport of trucks carrying goods. Articulation with other sectors of society had been a fundamental part of MTD's politics, which has resulted in coalitions to coordinate actions with peasant organizations, student groups, neighborhood assemblies, and other collectives. Internationally, they have shown a great interest in contacting other organizations and anti-capitalist experiences in other countries.

Also in Argentina, other workers found new ways to resist unemployment through direct action. Since 2001, more and more workers have refused to end up unemployed because a businessman feels like shutting down a business and relocating to a new place for increased profits. With the prospect of losing their jobs, many workers decided to occupy factories that were about to close or become abandoned, and start up production without a boss or owner, under a system of workers' self-management. The worker-controlled factory movement uses direct action with an organizational practice based on horizontalism and autonomy.

✖ CONTACTS
MTDs: *www.frentedariosantillan.org/fpds/*
Zanon (occupied factory): *www.obrerosdezanon.com.ar*

Women against exploitation and patriarchy: World March of Women

Many feminists believe that there is a broad relationship between the capitalist system, exploitation, and violence against women, especially in poor countries. This is why the Fédération des femmes du Québec formed in 1966 with the idea of carrying out an action that would connect struggles on an international level, and build a coalition with other sectors from society.

AFTER FIVE YEARS OF PREPARATION THE FIRST WORLD MARCH OF WOMEN TOOK PLACE IN 2000 WITH MORE THAN 6,000 ORGANIZATIONS FROM 161 COUNTRIES PARTICIPATING, DENOUNCING THE "DOUBLE EXPLOITATION" IMPOSED ON WOMEN BY CAPITALIST GLOBALIZATION AND PATRIARCHY.

The organizational structure of the WMW is based on the longtime experience of feminists' horizontal groups of reflection and exchanging of practices and knowledge, respect for the autonomy of each of these grass roots groups, regional and social diversity, popular education projects as a key in the strategies to gain equality between men and women, and the participation from all members in decision making.

The demands of WMW go beyond traditional feminist appeals, which have helped them to establish coalitions with the global resistance movement. The "fight against poverty" means, for the WMW, "to attack the domain of the ruling economic system: neoliberal capitalism" and to fight for "economic and social autonomy" of women. They question and challenge the policies of the World Bank, WTO, the IMF, and NATO. Their demands include the acknowledgment and remuneration of unpaid domestic work, the elimination of foreign debt, the "fair and equal distribution of the planet's resources," social control of financial markets, and demilitarization, etc.

THEY ALSO QUESTION THE *COMMODIFICATION* OF BODIES IN ADVERTISEMENTS, CUTBACKS IN PUBLIC SPENDING, AND THE FLEXIBILITY OF THE WORK FORCE, THREE CONCRETE WAYS IN WHICH CAPITALIST GLOBALIZATION HITS WOMEN.

The great success of the 2000 action pushed protestors to transform the WMW into a permanent network. They have planed international meetings and actions between 2000 and 2010.

✖ CONTACTS
www.worldmarchofwomen.org

Ecologists defend the planet and public spaces: Save the Narmada and Reclaim the Streets

One of the most devastating effects of capitalism has taken its toll on planet earth, destroying public spaces and nature. More and more environmentalists and defenders of public spaces have found common ground and linked their fight against capitalism. A good example is the *Save the Narmada River movement (Narmada Bachao Andolan NBA)*. NBA was created as a struggle of residents of the Narmada river valley in India against the construction of large dams on the Narmada River, destined to provide water to industrial areas.

THE DAMS WOULD HAVE MEANT THE DESTRUCTION OF THOUSANDS OF ACRES OF LAND AND THE CONSTANT DISPLACEMENT OF THOUSANDS OF RURAL RESIDENTS. IN ADDITION THE DAM WOULD DESTROY ALL NATURE SANCTUARIES, DISRUPTING THE ECOLOGICAL BALANCE IN THE REGION.

The creation of NBA in 1980 consolidated a wide coalition of organizations opposed to the dam construction, which include environmental organizations in India and other countries.

In a series of important direct actions and massive mobilizations, NBA was able to implement the idea that local residents have the right to participate in decisions that affect their environment, no matter if the decisions are made on a local, national, or even international level.

In fact, part of the international repercussions of NBA's struggle was that the World Bank—principal funder and supporter of the dam project—had to revise its policies and the way they make decisions to introduce policies. NBA forced the World Bank to include local residents in round table negotiations and to take into account environmental consequences before funding projects. Finally, NBA struggle was one of the first struggles to propose *sustainable development*, and demanded that women and men have the right to decide what investment projects are carried out and the kind of economic growth that is best for a community.

Another good example is *Reclaim the Streets* (RTS), formed in 1991 by a group of radical environmentalists, squatters, and alternative artists in London. The idea of RTS was simple: disrupt traffic with huge *surprise parties* in public throughways as a form of protest against the privatization of public spaces and pollution. RTS's first parties brought together more than 20,000 people, and soon the idea spread to other countries.

Creativity is fundamental to RTS and their party style is not an obstacle to their radical politics: in one of their most famous parties, activists from RTS pickaxed pavement on a London highway and planted trees as a way of sending the message, "Beneath the pavement…the forest!"

✖ **CONTACTS**
About NBA and other similar movements: *www.narmada.org*
RTS: *www.gn.apc.org/rts*

Immigrants challenge borders and racism: the No Borders network

Millions of people throughout the world migrate in search of better conditions in far-off lands, to face situations of super-exploitation and discrimination. To keep the *nomad multitudes* under control, capitalism has devised racism and severe repressive mechanisms. Through the Nation-States, capitalism limits the political rights of anyone classified as a *foreigner*. This is why more and more immigrants have begun to explore forms of organizing that go beyond (and reject) national identities. A good example is the *No Borders* (NB) network, which links antiracist and anti-capitalist collectives from all over Europe.

NB collaborates to organize "clandestine" or "undocumented" immigrants. Through direct actions and cultural interventions, they have attacked the "detention centers", concentration camps for illegal immigrants. Their actions call attention to the injustices "undocumented" men and women must face, such as not being able to move freely or having basic rights denied because they are considered "illegal."

One of their most famous actions are the "border camps" where activists and immigrants met near border areas to act against the border regime, temporarily blurring the "borders" or "lines" between nation-states.

THE LAND IS OURS

FREED OF MOVEM UR ALL CITI NS

WE ARE IMMIGRANTS, NOT CRIMINALS

Through their actions, the NB network has reintroduced the revolutionary idea of the global citizen, or the right of any person to have their political rights as citizens recognized wherever they are.

✖ CONTACTS
NB: *www.noborder.org/*

The Poor resist privatization: the Anti-privatization forum

The capitalist system survives because only a handful of people attain and concentrate resources, depriving and excluding everyone else from those resources.

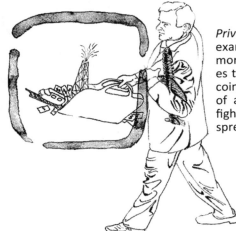

Privatization of public services, for example, implies that more and more people lose access to services to meet basic needs. It is not a coincidence why we find elements of anti-capitalist struggles in the fight against privatizations that has spread throughout the world.

A good example is the organizations that united in the *Anti-privatization forum* in South Africa (APF). Created in 2000, APF links unions, communities, activists, students, and Leftist parties to coordinate a struggle against privatizations and to demand a free supply of water and electricity for the poor. Part of their campaign consists of "the public exposition of capitalism's and the dominant classes' objectives," and the development of popular education workshops in communities.

The member organizations of APF developed some of the most celebrated *direct action* tactics in the world, like the famous Soweto "reconnection brigades," which provide illegal electric connections to residents who had their electricity disconnected because they could not pay.

The *Anti-Eviction Campaign* (AEC) in Cape Town is a horizontal organization made up of residents from poor neighborhoods. Its objective is to stop the evictions of residents who can't make mortgage payments to the banks. The direct action tactics of the AEC includes open resistance against evictions, the reinstatement of evicted families, and occupation of government buildings, among others.

While they struggle every day against capitalism in concrete ways, South Africans are building a "non-privatized" world with different kind of social relations.

✖ CONTACTS
APF: *www.apf.org.za*
AEC: *www.antieviction.org.za*

Alternative Media: from political art and the "communication guerrilla" to Indymedia

Capitalism tries to control the emission as well as the reception of messages on a daily basis. Capitalism limits access to information and gives power to the mass media through advertising or directly through corporate ownership of media. From the beginning, anti-capitalism made efforts to create new forms of communication that challenge *cultural control* by creating its own media and using art to transmit political ideas. Among more recent tactics, two have been to interfere advertising and to *subvert* corporate and State messages.

TWO EXAMPLES OF "COMMUNICATION GUERRILLA" INTERVENTIONS FROM THE CANADIAN GROUP *ADBUSTERS*.

Activists focused on these tactics of "culture jamming" or "pirate advertising," especially after the 1980s.

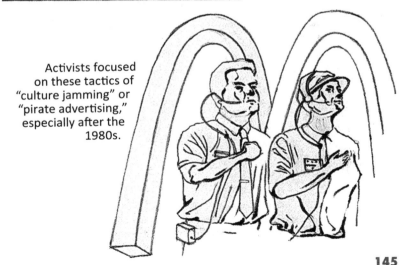

The internet has also allowed the number of sites and independent media organizations to multiply. The Indymedia network is probably one of the most emblematic examples. The first *Independent Media Center* (IMC) of the Indymedia network was set up in 1999 in Seattle to cover the protests against the WTO summit. Foreseeing that the mainstream press would not provide accurate coverage of the protests, a group of activists and independent journalists came up with the idea of creating an internet site where protestors could produce, edit, and distribute their own news content.

During the protest, the new website *Indymedia* received over a million visits, more than the corporate media sites like CNN. The immediate success made it clear the importance of creating independent alternative media outlets.

The idea of Indymedia combines the criteria of autonomy from the new anti-capitalism with the conception of participatory information. Indymedia sites are interactive: aside from media produced by Indymedia collectives, anyone can produce journalistic content and publish their own news. Even though each IMC functions autonomously and differently from location to location, many are organized in horizontal collectives made up of volunteer activists, and are open to participation from new volunteers. Media activists tend to establish strong relationships with social movements, sharing their media knowledge so that social activists can learn how to create and distribute their own media.

INDYMEDIA SITES

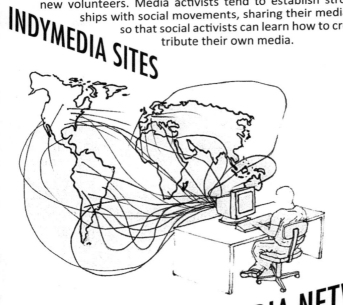

AN ALTERNATIVE MEDIA NETWORK

Quickly, Indymedia has become a trustworthy media outlet, and has transformed into a fundamental tool for social movements. Today there are hundreds of Indymedia sites in cities throughout the world, and millions of people use the site to publish news and get information.

✖ CONTACTS
Indymedia: www.indymedia.org
Adbusters: www.adbusters.org

Building networks of communication and action: The World Social Forum and other experiences

For many years many of the new anti-capitalist movements have created communication and coordination networks. There are many examples like the *People's Global Action* previously described or the *Direct Action Network*, which coordinates horizontal collectives that carry out actions in dozens of cities in the United States. Another way of coordinating actions are "campaigns" organized around specific issues.

Even though they don't always question the capitalist system, these *campaigns* against *specific* issues have been useful in criticizing the *entire* capitalist system, as well as relating anti-capitalist collectives with one another and to organize shared actions.

The experience of the World Social Forum (WSF) has contributed enormously to the communication between movements and organizations throughout the world. The first WSF was held in Porto Alegre, Brazil in January 2001, organized by a number of Brazilian and European organizations.

The WSF hoped to function as a parallel summit in opposition to the *World Economic Forum* in Davos, Switzerland, in which business leaders, heads of government and "gurus" of neoliberalism met. More than 15,000 activists, representatives from social movements, and intellectuals came together to exchange ideas during the first WSF, which exceeded initial expectations. Since the first meeting, the WSF has developed as a powerful space and tool for struggles to articulate together a shared global resistance.

At the second WSF, more than 50,000 people from all over the world participated in a week of intense debate. During that year, social forums were also held on a continental level, even by country, strengthening the exchange of ideas and experiences.

The third WSF was held in 2003, with more than 100,000 people participating. A *Social Movements International Network* was proposed to link struggles throughout the world in a more permanent way.

Since its formation, the WSF has received criticisms from the movement. Even though it didn't set out to have a single political program, grassroots movements have questioned the persistence of hierarchical and nontransparent practices from within the WSF, as well as the close ties to organizations and NGOs that do not advocate a non-capitalist society, but simply "humanize" the current system. Although the WSF continues to be a productive event for anti-capitalists, many have sought out alternative spaces.

✖ **CONTACTS**
PGA: *www.nadir.org/nadir/initiativ/agp/en/*
FSM: *www.forumsocialmundial.org.br*

A movement of movements:
The Battle of Seattle and Global Action Days

The networks of social movements and organizations that resist capitalism multiply and grow every day. Some believe that a *movement of global resistance* exists, a true "movement of movements" which, although incipient, is able to coordinate actions globally.

MAY OUR RESISTANCE BE AS GLOBAL AS CAPITAL

The media tends to call it the "anti-globalization movement" and its participants, "global-phobic." But this characterization is wrong. Almost no one is against globalization per se, but against *capitalist* globalization. In fact, many activists prefer to call the movement the "global movement" or "alter-globalization" movement.

Global Action Days (GAD) are a good example of the beginnings of global coordination. A GAD is an action organized by coalitions of groups and movements from different places around the globe, and that can be carried out in several cities at the same time, or when activists from different countries meet at the same place. These coalitions reflect the moments in which the loose networks that connect us solidify in a specific focal articulation to carry out a specific action.

A good example is the Battle of Seattle in November 1999. For more than a year, dozens of groups worked hard to organize a massive direct action: to prevent a meeting of the World Trade Organization (WTO) that wanted to introduce more extensive free trade and greater suffering for workers in poor countries. Many of the participating groups articulated themselves through "spokesperson councils" made up of several hundred people to discuss and plan the action in a horizontal way.

FINALLY, CLOSE TO 40,000 PEOPLE PROTESTED IN SEATTLE.

DURING THREE DAYS OF CONFRONTATIONS WITH THE POLICE, THREE DAYS OF ENDURING INTENSE REPRESSION, PROTESTERS WERE ABLE TO STOP THE WTO FROM MEETING.

Another success of the *Battle of Seattle* was that through the action a wide array of social subjects were mobilized: unions, environmental groups, socialists and anarchists, Third World workers and consumers from the First World, farmers and artists, feminists and indigenous, all from dozens of different countries, all "united by one no, and many yeses." The *Battle of Seattle* inspired thousands of women and men to keep fighting around the globe. The following Global Action Days grew with enthusiasm.

THE FIRST DAYS OF GLOBAL ACTION

✖ **Prague, September 26, 2000**
Against the IMF and World Bank meetings

✖ **Quebec, April 20-22, 2001**
Against the Summit of the Americas and the Free Trade Agreement of the Americas (FTAA) in Quebec

✖ **Genoa, Italy July 15-22, 2001**
Against the G8 meetings

✖ **February 15, 2003:** millions march in hundreds of cities against the war in Iraq

The anti-summit actions have forced the powerful to meet behind police fences and in places impossible to access, like a mountain top in Canada or an autocracy in Qatar.

There's been a debate about the GDAs. Some think that anti-summit protests aren't effective, because they haven't had the same success as Seattle. On the contrary, they argue that the "movement of movements" should put more energy in fortifying the *local* struggles, organizations, and networks.

No "programs," but lots of ideas

In the media, the spokespeople of the powerful often tell us that we are fighting for an impossible utopia, that we have good intentions but no concrete proposals.

The new anti-capitalism doesn't have a single, closed "program," and maybe will never have one. But this doesn't mean that the movement doesn't have concrete ideas about how to change the world.

Ideas that circulate in global networks

In the endless "conversation" taking place throughout the global networks, there are many proposals of how to change the world in very concrete ways. Some are promoted by only the anti-capitalists; others are shared even by those who only want to make capitalism "more humane." Some could be applied today; others require the construction of a *counter-power* to sustain the proposals. What is important is that there are alternatives out there; and they can provide answers to some of the globe's most serious problems.

What follows are some concrete proposals. Surely, many of them won't be enough to "change the world" on their own. But it is good to show that there are also proposals for *partial* change and changes that could be introduced in the short term, and not just because they work out best for the powerful. Toward the end of this section, we include some projects for *integral* change, for the creation of a non-capitalist society, free from exploitation and oppression.

Some proposals for partial change

REDISTRIBUTION OF GLOBAL INCOME

There are several concrete proposals for the immediate transfer of wealth from the richest to the poorest countries, and to at least partially cease super-exploitation of the Third World in the short term.

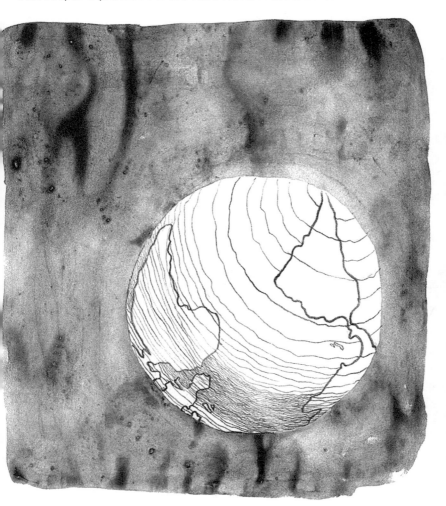

PROPOSALS

✖ Immediate cancellation of foreign debt and the abolition of the IMF

✖ Standards of "fair trade," so that rich countries pay a higher price for Third World products

✖ Abolition of "export processing zones" in which corporations profit from semi-slave conditions of the workforce in the poorest countries

✖ Creation of labor standards that can be applied globally (prohibition of child labor, universal regulations for safe working conditions, and a universal work day, etc.)

✖ Transnational unionization of workers, especially if they work for the same corporation, to avoid companies from going overseas for lower paid workers

✖ **FOR MORE INFORMATION ON CAMPAIGNS AGAINST FOREIGN DEBT**
www.odiousdebts.org
www.jubileesouth.org/

CONTROL OVER MOVEMENT OF CAPITAL

Free movement of capital causes increasing suffering for most of humanity. There are several initiatives to change this situation in the short term.

PROPOSALS

✖ Creation of laws that impose restrictions on speculative financial transactions

✖ Abolition of "fiscal paradises" and secret bank accounts used to avoid taxes and to "launder" money

✖ Giving workers the ability to decide how their retirement and pension funds are used. In many cases, these funds are administered by financial companies, which invest the money in projects that hurt workers.

✖ Creation of "responsible savings" standards, which allow citizens to tell banks how they should invest their deposits

✖ **MORE INFORMATION ON THE CONTROL OVER THE MOVEMENT OF CAPITAL AND FAIR TRADE**
www.bicusa.org
www.globalexchange.org
www.attac.org

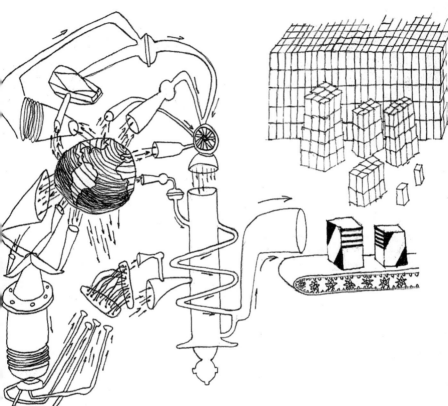

→ There are a number of initiatives to stop the alarming level of environmental destruction and to move forward with *sustainable development*. For example, impose punitive fines for Nations that allow the destruction of natural resources that are patrimony of humanity (like the air) or the creation of tax and commercial standards to increase the use of unharmful products for the environment. There are people who argue that companies should take immediate responsibility for the environmental damage that they have caused, and that society should demand the right to democratically decide what type of technology and consumption should be permitted. There are even "primitivist" arguments that call for the return of preindustrial technological standards.

Increasingly more and more transgenic seeds, fertilizers, and pesticides are being used in farming, which destroy the earth, threaten public health, and curtail farmers' sovereignty as they become more dependent on multinational corporations for food production. And increasingly, more people are opposed to this kind of agriculture. Many organizations, farmers, and citizens have called for the defense of *food sovereignty,* or the right for communities to be able to feed themselves from local food production. Many groups also promote the use of agro-ecological technology on a small scale, more labor-intensive than capital-intensive.

✖ **MORE INFORMATION ON ECOLOGY**
www.ambiental.net
www.insurgentdesire.org.uk
www.agroeco.org
www.grain.org
www.eco-action.org

BASIC INCOME

Today's societies are in the position to guarantee a universal minimal monthly income, for every person, on the basis that they are human beings, regardless or not if they are "employed." In this way, the minimal living costs for survival would be covered.

I'M NOT FORCED TO WORK UNDER ANY CONDITIONS JUST SO I WON'T STARVE. NOW, I'M GOING TO WORK WHEREVER I WANT TO.

MORE INFORMATION ON BASIC INCOME
www.basicincome.org/bien/

Global citizenship

PLANET EARTH PASSPORT

Global citizenship would mean extending political and civil rights to all men and women, regardless of where they were born. All human beings should have the same rights, independent of where they live, and they should have freedom to move and live in any part of the world. This would mean the abolition of the national *apartheid*, border restrictions, visa requirements, passports, etc.

163

PARTICIPATORY DEMOCRACY / DIRECT DEMOCRACY

There are several proposals for alternatives for representative institutions and electoral political systems, which would allow for greater participation from the population. The *participatory budget* used in Porto Alegre and other cities, which has allowed citizens to directly decide on how to spend part of the city budget, is one example. There are other examples that go even further, and propose forms of *direct democracy* without delegation—especially on a municipal or regional level—through council and assembly systems. Anarchist author Murray Bookchin's "libertarian municipalism" or professor Stephen Shalom's "participatory politics" are particularly interesting.

✖ **MORE INFORMATION ABOUT PARTICIPATORY DEMOCRACY**
www.zcommunications.org/zspace/stephenshalom
www.communalism.net/
www.social-ecology.org

NONCOMMERCIAL EXCHANGE

A large part of current production, especially computers, design, communication, entertainment, personal care, etc., are produced collectively and are transmitted digitally, without any material production costs. This is what is called "immaterial labor," which makes up an important part of production in today's society.

✖ MATERIAL PRODUCTS

✖ IMMATERIAL PRODUCTS

Many have proposed for "immaterial labor" to be exchanged freely, freeing this production from the rules of the market and private property. There is an important movement of *free software* and *Copy Left* products, so if someone wants to copy the media or product it can be done for *free*, without anyone making claims to the intellectual property.

A number of social movements are developing forms of exchange outside of the market. For example, many are experimenting with *local currency* that increases the acquisition of goods produced locally and on a small scale.

Some proposals for integral change

Beyond proposals for partial change, how can we organize a free and egalitarian society which isn't based on exploitation and oppression? The spirit of many of the partial changes commented upon synthesize some of the proposals for *integral* change, which aspire to create a society completely organized upon non-capitalist norms.

IT'S CLEAR THAT WE WANT A SOCIETY BASED ON THE VALUES OF EQUALITY, SOLIDARITY, RESPECT FOR THE ENVIRONMENT, PLURALISM, AND FREEDOM. WE DON'T WANT SOCIAL CLASSES, OR DIVISIONS BETWEEN LEADERS AND FOLLOWERS.

BUT THE MOST DIFFICULT QUESTION TO ANSWER IS: HOW DO WE ORGANIZE AN ECONOMY THAT'S BETTER THAN CAPITALISM?

The new anti-capitalism seeks to build a society free from ownership of the means of production, but radically different from the centralized, hierarchical and state based model that the traditional Left has proposed following the Soviet model. Some have proposed *market socialism* that would combine mechanisms of the market with decentralized state economic planning.

167

Others completely reject the idea that the market should be maintained in a non-capitalist society, or that the State should be in charge of planning. Michael Albert (1947-) for example, has designed a complex system for a *participatory economy* (or "parecon").

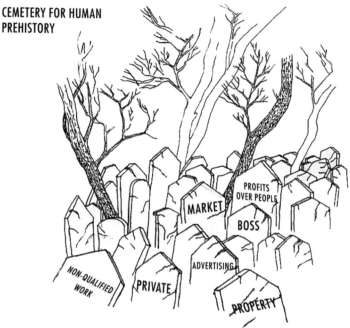

CEMETERY FOR HUMAN PREHISTORY

PROFITS OVER PEOPLE

MARKET

BOSS

NON-QUALIFIED WORK

PRIVATE

ADVERTISING

PROPERTY

In a *participatory economy* there would be no bosses, businessmen, or private property. All workers would receive remuneration according to their efforts and they would share disempowering or manual tasks. Production planning and consumption would be carried out democratically and in a decentralized organizational structure, without using market mechanisms or bureaucratic leadership. Every worker and consumer would make decisions about investments, production, and consumption together in their community, *horizontally*. Workers would be in charge of *participatory planning* and consumers would meet in a council system that would function on a local level, as well as on a regional and national level.

✖ MORE INFORMATION ABOUT PARTICIPATORY ECONOMY
http://www.zcommunications.org/topics/parecon

Open ending

Index

Index of names

Acknowledgements

This book wouldn't have been possible without the extraordinary people with whom I had the opportunity to share experiences in activism. In particular, my compañeros from the Cid Campeador Popular Assembly, with whom I learned many of the ideas that this book offers. My fellow activist compañeros from Intergaláctika and the magazine El Rodaballo were also strong sources of inspiration.

I'd especially like to thank the Ilustradores Unidos for their talent and dedication.

I confess that I have stolen more than one idea from my friends Horacio Tarcus, Martín Bergel, and Franco Ingrassia.

E.A.

The Ilustradores Unidos would like to thank Pitu, Zulema, Laura, Intergaláctika, and the compañeros from the Taller Popular de Serigrafía (Popular Silkscreen Workshop) for their generous contribution and support.

We dedicate these illustrations to the protagonists from the anti-capitalist struggles in our country, in particular the assemblies, unemployed workers movements, the workers from the recuperated factories, and everyone who protests in the streets.

The authors

Ezequiel Adamovsky (Buenos Aires, 1971) is an activist and anti-capitalist writer. He has published numerous articles and essays in newspapers, books, and magazines in Argentina and other countries. He has participated as a lecturer in diverse workshops and academic and political gatherings.

He completed his undergraduate studies at the University of Buenos Aires and later received his PhD in History from the UCL/University of London.

Leo Rocco, Diego Posadas, Pablo Rosales, Magdelena Jitrik, Horacio Abram Lujan, and Mariela Scafati illustrated this book. They are visual artists who participate in the Taller Popular de Serigrafía, a group that formed during the intense upsurge of political and social movements during the popular rebellion of December 2001. They formed with the objective of stamping images of support, artistic, and political accompaniment to all kinds of protests.